The Book of Amazing People

Research: James Miller, Helen Sykes, Melanie Jarvis-Vaughan, Peter Guthridge, Mark Gregory and Shawn Willis

Edited By Kizzi Nkwocha (c)

Published by Mithra Publishing 2015

Sponsored by Voila Success. The best place on the planet for brilliant success books. Visit Voila Success at www.voilasuccess.com

Optimism is the faith that leads to achievement. Nothing can be done without hope and confidence.

Helen Keller

Trust yourself. Create the kind of self that you will be happy to live with all your life. Make the most of yourself by fanning the tiny, inner sparks of possibility into flames of achievement.

Golda Meir

Achievement of your happiness is the only moral purpose of your life, and that happiness, not pain or mindless self-indulgence, is the proof of your moral integrity, since it is the proof and the result of your loyalty to the achievement of your values.

Ayn Rand

The amazing people showcased in this book

Tara Scammell	Gordon Rutty
Nikki Galagher	Karen Chaston
Missy Robinson	Ted Gunnarsson
Craig Merrett	Judy Sahay
Stella Gianotto	Ashley Stamatinos
Gareth Craven	Sandy Hobley
Sarah Cordiner	Luke Sheedy
Felena Hanson	Melissa Madgwick
Janeen Sonsie	

Introduction

Welcome to The Book of Amazing People, a ground-breaking project that honours and showcases individual success and achievement.

In the chapters of this book you will read inspiring and motivating real-life stories of ordinary people making their lives truly extraordinary. Some of our contributors have overcome loss, serious illness and heartache. Many have transformed their lives through physical and emotional change while others have established successful businesses against the odds. Hopefully by reading this book you will have an insight into what success means to you and how to achieve it.

When researching the stories for The Book of Amazing People, a book which, hopefully will be the first in a series, we asked ourselves three key questions: What internal characteristics do these individuals possess and what external factors have been present in their lives? What advice do they have to help ordinary people build personal strengths to overcome the challenges they face?

By answering these questions, I hope The Book of Amazing People will provide valuable insights that will help you learn to lead a *self-determined* life. But what is self-determination? There are many definitions to choose from. The following definition – and my personal favourite - incorporates a number of common themes found in other definitions.

Self-determination is a combination of skills, knowledge, and beliefs that enable a person to engage in goal-directed, self-regulated, autonomous behaviour. An understanding of one's strengths and limitations together with a belief in oneself as capable and effective are essential to self-determination.

I believe gaining control over your life involves learning and then successfully applying a number of self-determination skills, such as goal setting, understanding your abilities and disabilities, problem solving, and self-advocacy. The personal process of learning, using, and self-evaluating these skills in a variety of settings is at the heart of self-determination. It is also at the heart of The Book of Amazing People. Read. Learn. Succeed.

Kizzi

About Kizzi Nkwocha

Kizzi Nkwocha is the editor of My Making Money Magazine, Next Gen Trader and My Entrepreneur Magazine. He made his mark in the UK as publicist, journalist and social media pioneer.

As a widely respected and successful media consultant Nkwocha has represented a diverse range of clients including the King of Uganda, mistresses of President Clinton, Amnesty International, Pakistani cricket captain Wasim Akram, campaign group Jubilee 2000, Dragons Den businessman, Levi Roots and world record teenage sailor, Michael Perham.

Nkwocha has also become a well-known personality on both radio and television. He has been the focus of a Channel 4 documentary on publicity and has hosted his own talk show, London Line, on Sky TV.

He also co-presented a weekly current affairs program in Spain on Radio Onda Cero International and both radio and TV shows in Cyprus.

His books have included the fiction novel, Heavens Fire, the business guide books: Business, Business, Business!, Mind Your Own Business, Insiders Know-How: Public Relations and the international bestseller SocMed: Social Media For Business. He also runs a successful agency called Social Biz Training which trains people to use social media for business. His agency site is at www.socialbiztraining.com

Follow Kizzi on Twitter: https://twitter.com/kizzinkwocha

Overcoming Difficulties by Believing in Yourself

(Editor's note – At the authors request this chapter has been left justified to accommodate readers with Dyslexia)

This story starts way back beyond birth. Long before you were even conceived your blueprint was already taking form. As your ancestors made their way through their lives, your genetic makeup was in the pipeline. This is exactly the same for all of us. Your ability to learn and understand your education comes from what you inherit from your parents.

In this opening chapter of the Book of Amazing People I'm going to give you a little insight into my world, a world of colour and energy, a world where I have a unique set of strategies to connect and interact on a daily basis. There is a lot that happens behind the scenes in my daily life and you may at times see reflections into your own world. If you do, let me encourage you to believe in yourself. Your journey is unique and so is your gift for that matter. Take the time to consider what you know and who you are because you have a very individual purpose for being here. You are important and your life is divinely appointed for this time in history.
My genetic blueprint set in motion an understanding which very few get to experience. To the "normal" world I have learning issues. But I know a thing or two about "learning issues" and if you'll give me thirty minutes of your time I'd like to share some of what I know. You see learning issues are both genetic and trauma based. They become a part of your DNA as a consequence of your parents and at times from the stress and trauma which life takes you through.

In my case the condition which has caused me the most difficulty is visual dyslexia. For me that means when I look at a page of text, the words move in many different patterns. So reading and comprehending words was one of my worst nightmares. Do you remember having to stand in front of the whole class and read out loud? I would always be violently sick. My nerves would be on edge worrying about getting it wrong and being laughed at. This would kick my dyslexia in to high speed and the words would spin out of control giving me a feeling like vertigo. It was a traumatic panic attack, and made me feel faint and weak in every part of my body.

I knew all the feelings but what I didn't know was the why I felt this way. Looking at the other kids showed me this didn't happen to them. Why me? I thought.

This did three things in my head...

1. It caused destructive self-talk
2. It turned me into a detective, a Sherlock Holmes. (Did you know Sherlock was an Aspie?)
3. I was determined to understand the weakness and the strength of "why me"!

When I was about seven years old my dyslexia really kicked in. Because I had just arrived in Australia from the UK, I thought it was the text (or font). I decided it was a cultural thing. I didn't find out it was dyslexia until I was about 22 years old. I discovered this when I took my two daughters for an eye test and a hearing test. In my mind I was thinking they were not going to suffer like I had.

Now I know you are probably thinking 'why didn't my parents do something about my learning issues?' The answer is simple. I was just like them so it wasn't seen as any kind of disability or learning issue, it was just seen as my struggle to learn, and the same as both my parents had. The truth is... this is what drew them to each other; they felt safe together because they understood each other.

They understood each other enough to communicate and strengthen each other's weakness so Mum did the spelling and Dad did the maths.

Mum's self talk was, "I am not good enough" and Dad's self talk was, "I will find a way to understand what ever is put in front of me". You can now see where I got the concept of becoming a detective.

Before I take you on a journey into the unpacking of learning issues let me share with you what I have and how each one has its inabilities, amazing strengths and beautiful attributes.

Yes you have it right, I am in love with what the world sees as learning issues or challenges.

In fact I have what is known as a cohort (in the sense of a band or gathering) of learning issues. (But sometimes they act more like accomplices and compatriots and gang up on me.☺)

Here's the list...

*   **Visual dyslexia**. At least 6 different reading patterns.
*   **Auditory dyslexic**. I hear at a 100% but my ability to process what I hear is around 70%.

- **Dyscalculia**. (Maths) I cannot add up or do any maths in my head and times tables just don't compute in my head at all.
- **Dyspraxia**. (Motor co-ordination) This means I can be clumsy and have trouble speaking. In my case the right side of my tongue moves or is lazy when I'm tired or stressed so words don't come out clear. This makes it impossible to use Speech recognition software. If I close my eyes I have no point of reference giving me balance issues (I have now overcome this). Dyspraxia affects everything that involves both sides of my body, Eg. Crawling as a baby.
- **Irlen**. (Light sensitivity) Also known as Scotopic Sensitivity Syndrome. It means lights and even sunlight play a huge role in me being able to think, read and learn. I am presently studying community services and to study I have to plan when, where and how much I can learn on any given day.
- **Synesthesia**. I see things in front and to the side of me in colours. Eg. Words that someone is speaking. Billy Joel is synesthetic. He sees music in front of him so instead of it being inside his head he sees it in a flow in front of him and he writes it from there.
- **Spacial dyslexia**. No real sense of distance, so the GPS can say turn in 800 metres and I have no idea what that looks like. I can use light posts because they are a set distance apart, but if I'm on a highway there are no poles to count and I could miss a turn off. I need points of reference.
- **Dysgraphia**. This is how you write and hold a pen. You see how you hold a pen and where the pressure is makes a huge difference in how the messaging coming down your arm into your hands is processed. If you do a job where you are required to stand, you will stand in a way that makes it easy to write but it can cause RSI and lower back problems and much more.
- **Attention Deficit Disorder**. ADD is my best and worst gift. Under control I work incredibly fast and think very fast on my feet, but at its worst I have no ability to hold thoughts and work with them. It fights me when I want to stay still and concentrate on conversations and causes me to butt in because I already know

where you are going. I want to answer you before I forget what I need or want to say.

- **Sensitive Person Syndrome**. Yes this is a real condition and because of my inabilities to learn in the normal ways this trait got heightened. I have learned to use this to my advantage. Sensitive person syndrome means you are sensitive to everything around you and the environment you are in. If I am not careful you can misinterpret the meaning behind my actions. For example: If I fold my arms towards you, you might decide I am shutting you out, but what I am actually doing is hugging myself in re-assurance because I'm in overload. I have to always be physically aware of every part of my body language. I also see everything you do, from the way you hold your head to your eyes, nose and the flaring of you nostrils, to your mouth, shoulders, how hard your foot hits the floor as you walk; I sense everything. This means as I said earlier, I have to be aware of possible overwhelm from the input of everything around me. Some days are awesome and some days are a battle with the constant awareness of a meltdown. It's a fine balance at times.
- **Obsessive Compulsive Disorder**. For me to control my life so I can learn and appear normal I am very OCD. This applies to where I sit, what time I do things in a day, to how much sleep I must have. Nothing in my life is by chance. The bad side to the OCD is there is never a day that is as perfect as I try and make it to be without impacting on another person's world, so I have learnt to be flexible in my OCD.
- **Aspergers**. Yes, I sit there too. I have a lot of Aspergers traits. What triggered me to look further at this trait is I don't have a funny bone in my body. I am very serious most of the time. Some of this is because I think I am constantly monitoring myself so I don't have a meltdown. This means that I don't give myself a break to enjoy life. (This is something which I am now working on)
- **3d thinking**. I can see something in my mind and keep turning it and explain every angle on it simply through my minds eye. Let's use a rose for instance. I will smell its perfume, feel the thorns and

its texture, see the slight veins in the leaves and the petals, see the delicate colour in the petals and how they fold down, etc. All of these senses happen as if it were a physical rose in my hand.

- **Executive function**. My thought process and actions are instantaneous. Basically If I can think it then I can do it. It's a childlike feature. A child will run to the play ground with no consideration that there is a busy road to be crossed to get to the park. The fallout from our actions can at times be very dangerous. The advantage to this is all things are possible, so we just make it happen.

I often joke that I slide up and down the spectrum of learning issues from one day to the next but the truth is it can be as fast as hour to hour due to sensory overload.

I tell the people I work with that you would never give a learning issue or disability to a weak person, it would break them in one day. It's hard work to appear normal.

What does normal look like anyway? Well, everyone with any disability is an expert on this subject because we have to watch, copy, imitate, control and manage everything from actions, melt downs, overload and much more, just so we don't give ourselves away.

People just do what they do without a thought, but that is not the case when you don't want to stand out from the crowd.

People with ADD and ADHD have to be so careful not to take over and look bossy, controlling, rude or abrupt. They often look like they are self centred; only interested in hearing their own voice and opinions which makes conversation hard work.

For the Aspie, they know that body language is 70% of the message and they struggle to communicate in that space. Tone is 27% and only 3% of the message is what is said.

For me, because of trying to listen to what is being said and the body language I need to read, one conversation can do me in for the rest of the day. If it is in a coffee shop with coffee grinders and milk frothers going off, conversations on other tables and the sounds of spoons, cutlery and cash registers for example, I have to constantly filter my conversation to make sure I don't break in mid sentence. All this input can cause my ADD to kick in and take you down multiple paths of conversation. If that happens you will feel totally lost and have no idea what I am talking about. Also, the lights and the music coming through the speakers and the movement in the room all come into my brain as valid information. It's a mutli-sensory overload. So a coffee and a conversation is pure hard work.

You see, whatever I do I am fully engaged because I have to be. I understand the effort people go to just to appear normal in a conversation. You would be surprised just how many people do this every day.

We all know the saying, the glass is half full or half empty? This drives my OCD mad! Either fill the glass or empty it. But I do understand the concept behind it and I have to reason with my brain every time I hear this statement. The way I think is very black and white with splashes of colour everywhere. A glass half full for me is completely full. I am both fully engaged, front and centre and balanced or I am not engaged at all, null and void. Splashes of colour represent how we have mastered the outcomes. The colours are either dark and stormy or bright and dancing (the synesthesia is kicking in).

Let me unpack for you my so called dys abilities which give me the most divine assets. I am now a Talent and Traits Analyst. I am able to see via the colours that come from your words and body language, how you see the world and your disabilities.

I spent my life up until I turned 50 handling them. They were amazing colours in the playground in my head, but outside that I wanted nothing more than to appear normal. Its human nature to feel like we belong, but each time I appeared abnormal I was cast aside and felt like I didn't fit. My aim now in life is to let the world see that people like me do fit. We were specially designed with out of the box thinking and out of the box abilities. With these out of the box abilities come traits that need to be harnessed and mastered to be our strength.

ADD and ADHD thinking is fast and full of ideas... the same for dyslexics. But the follow through on the ideas is shocking. This is because once thought of and we have it mapped out in our heads, we are bored and need the next new thing. So the question is how do we harness our creativity and make it work for us. Sir Richard Branson has mastered this. He thinks it and hands it over to his staff to put all the structures behind it. In his mind he gives them a complete picture of how it looks and works and his staff put it all in place. For me, my husband and a great team of people around me help me to put the concepts I design in place.

When I first embarked on this journey I meet a famous Australian copywriter who is my husband's mentor. After a Makers Mark bourbon or two, Sandy (full of courage) asked Mr. Pete Godfrey what made you get into copywriting. As he told his story I understood not only what he was saying but what he wasn't saying and I feed it back to him. Poor Pete blushed (and he will kill me for saying that here) but Pete knew how to flip things on their head, a gem I now use.

All information is not straight information. There is just as much information or maybe even more given in what's not actually said. The question I ask myself is, "What If I flip it?"

So for all the nasty traits of learning issues what is the flip side?

And that is what my business and my life's mission has now become.

Everything in life is a gem if you flip it (thanks Mr Pete Godfrey).

My mentor is Mr Pat Mesiti. Pat is just like me and showed me everything is possible if you have a dream and work out how YOU are going to bring it to life.

Pat causes me to dream and Pete teaches me how to put my dreams in print.

Now I don't care whether the label should be a mentor or a coach. I will only connect with people who have walked in my shoes. For me to learn I need information with multiple layers. I have an issue with leaders who know the information but have not lived it. If I am going to help people like me they need to know I have walked a mile in their shoes. This is because we believe people who we see as credible, that's how we learn.

That's why maths and English are hard to learn because you cannot live them. People like me need to smell, taste, feel, experience and so much more to understand.

People with dyslexia seem to work in pictures, films, codes and grids. They need layers of information to suit the way their brain processes. Dyslexic people are highly visual. I explain it to people like we speak two languages. Firstly there is English which we hear and then we need to convert it to dyslexic.

What do I mean? Here's an example. You have your birth language; let's say "Italian" and you learn a second language, "English". Unless you have a clear comprehension of the English language you need to convert it back to your native language being Italian. It's the same for dyslexics. They need time to convert back to their native dyslexic speak to understand how to gather and hold the information.

My business has become unpacking how people learn so they can better understand themself and understand how to position themselves in ways to be able to pick up all the learning's they want to learn.

You see, we now use multi sensory teaching methods for kids in the school systems, which is great. If the child can't learn in one way they have a chance to pick the information up in another. It's still not a 100% though. I know because my grand kids have learning issues and they are still struggling.

I am an avid studier and I am studying community services at the moment. Next, I will be going on to study counselling. In previous years I have studied Business and Training and Assessment in Education (TAE). The reason I am telling you this is to say I have learnt to understand how I need information. I have studied a number of times in the classroom and now I am studying online. Both ways have their advantages and their disadvantages for a dyslexic.

For many years (50 in fact) I thought I was dumb and just didn't understand but as soon as I embraced my dyslexia and decided to love it rather than keep it separated from me, I was able to learn to harness all the strength and beauty within the learning issues. It is still in my life but it has joined the party and now celebrates being a whole person.

This is what I now teach. It's like saying I hate my right arm, yet your right arm is the one that feeds you, and you have struggled on with your left arm for years.

Because I understand this concept and have learnt for myself from my own experience; my pain has been my greatest gain. You see, people are willing to be vulnerable with me. They know I understand them so they can come out of hiding knowing they can talk from a safe place.

I help people understand their good days, their bad days and much more. I talk about everything from sleep to foods, vitamins, feelings of overwhelm and all the reasons why they struggle to hold themselves together.

I talk to heaps of people with learning issues and the common thread through all of us is there was a time in our lives when we decided we just couldn't do the learning thing. For me that was 7 years old. I was very aware of what I could and couldn't learn and just would not try to go past that point. For some it's 9 years old, some 11 years old, it all depends on the level of disabilities and the language break down as I term it. In other words, the ability to convert what was being taught in to dyslexic language. Now I am saying dyslexic but it's whatever the learning difference is.

What this does from the evidence I am seeing so far is lock the emotions. You seem to be stuck in a time vacuum. It's like there is a standing point of safety and if you cross that line you could have a meltdown. People tell me they draw a line in the sand and even if they take a step over that line they will always keep one foot behind the line for safety.

Now this may not be everybody but it is everybody I have spoken to. I work mostly with people who have been in domestic violence but I also work as an adviser to an RTO for training courses on lots of different fields, with numbers of trainers who train in many different aspects. I also assist at East Coast Apprenticeships who ran the first ever dyslexic program (in Australia) in the field of the building trades which has now been opened up to all learning issues.

I also built on to an already existing program accepted by education Queensland called the Academy of Young Entrepreneurs (AYE) program. My version of the program is called the AYE Family Renewal Program. I have also built the L.O.V.E. Program which is an acronym for Leverage Over Valued Emotions. This program shows people how to use their emotions in a valuable way both in their personal lives and their business lives. Recently I have been working with the Inside Outside Theatre group putting a play together to show what it is like living in a household of learning issues. The good, the bad, the miscommunication etc. It will be an insight into how learning issues affect everyday lives.
Needless to say everything takes money so I am the fund raiser for these projects too. In wanting to reach and help people, I have been training myself to wear many hats in my business. There isn't a day when I am not learning something new.

This book is about amazing people and what they have contributed to this world. For a couple of days that's what I unpacked. I wondered what drives a person to do that, to work long hours and break boundaries... to stretch themselves further than they've ever been before?
What I came up with is they are a lover of mankind, for justice, for truth, and the belief that we are all interconnected. It's about the bible verse, "Love one another as God loves you" and in all religions we are taught to love and respect each other, to help bring the best out in each other.
As I struggle daily through life, I remember as a child I just wanted to be understood and valued for who I was, my strengths and my weaknesses, but mainly not to be made to feel like a failure. This is now what I do in my work.
I explain the beauty within learning issues, how ever they look, for each person. As an avid studier of human behaviours, I see each person struggle daily. That is, neuro-typicals, those with learning issues, health issues and social issues. If judgement stopped and compassion would rise, I believe people's hearts would flourish, teenage suicide would lower and comfort eating would reduce leading to less health issues. People with social issues,

where people don't know how to have friends and be connected, would be understood and instead of being forever outside the circle of friends, they'll be in the centre of friendships.

You see I believe if we think about the layers in people's minds and hearts rather than their actions and inabilities we will be stretched outside our own comfort zones into better places.

It's human nature! We just want to belong.

- We buy a house in a certain suburb because it aesthetically meets our needs and desires.
- The community of people who live there seem to act and think like us.
- We work in places with people who like the same work as us.
- We chat at the school our children attend and join sporting clubs etc.

People want to belong and to feel part of the connected group.

What has this got to do with the work I do?

It has to do with me explaining that just because English (reading and writing) or Maths are not your strong points, don't disconnect from the world. It took me until I was 50 to realise that despite my reading and writing difficulties I could still write emails (it can take me up to five hours to write one email) and use social media. I know I make mistakes. Gosh, this chapter has been completely scrutinised and edited by my copywriter husband. I just don't let the difficulty define me.

You see, if you struggle to read and these days you need to read to get a job (and for sending emails), people don't want to hire you. But if you look at all the other amazing qualities you have you will see why they *should* hire you. The interactive and creative skills are really heightened when these academic skills are subdued.

Reading and writing is only one part of life's skill set and yet it's made out to be everything in life. People are even judged by it. Just look at school reports. By the way, lots of artists are dyslexic 3D thinkers and they are super creative. But if you judged them purely by the way they read or write, you would completely miss their capability. It's a bit like judging a fish by its ability to climb a tree.

You know, 3d thinkers can design a building in their mind's eye and give you every detail of that building. Yet this person could get overlooked at a job interview because they struggle to fill in the paper work. They also appear way too nervous and all over the shop with their thoughts. In dyslexia managing nerves and stress and trying to appear normal takes a huge amount of work, so please give consideration to people that are not interacting well with questions and answers. Instead have a conversation and let them explain how they function and you will see them in a very different light.

People with ADD and ADHD struggle to sit still and need to move to talk, learn and process. You may meet someone that needs to move but knows they must sit still or they will be discredited. That uses so much of their energy. They will give you their best when you understand how they work. Let me give you an example from a Recruitment agency. The boss lady said she had to let two grown men go because they never did what she asked them to do or would do the last thing she had told them to do. In her words "they would procrastinate".

Once I explained their behaviours she was very sad. She realised she had let two good men go because they never told her what was happening for them. I asked her if she had ever asked them how they needed to receive information. She answered no.
Because of this experience I now teach workshops in that organisation and that is one of the main questions I get people to ask. You might say, "I am the boss. They need to do it my way". But as leaders or bosses we need to build strong working teams with the goal of looking after our business and our work force. If you care, your employees will care.

There's an old saying: People don't care how much you know until they know how much you care. If we were all to adopt this principle in the workforce, from the interview room to the seasoned long term employee, I believe the world would be a very different place.
If you are one of the misunderstood fragile souls who feel they don't fit, cut yourself some slack. You have a wealth of knowledge and inherent understanding within you. Your gift is designed for this time in history and needs to be available to the wider community.

Sure you might make mistakes and feel you didn't succeed but I want you to know that lack of success is not the end. It just gives you a launch point for your next move.
Thomas Edison made something like 10,000 mistakes. His response was he knew 10,000 ways not to make a light bulb. It would be a dark world if he didn't keep trying.

Believe in yourself and stay the course. You will get there if you persist. I know because I have had more successes in the last few years than I have in my whole life.
And if I can... I believe you can too.

Sandy Hobley

About the author

Sandy is the founder of Embracing Dyslexia.

After having dealt with learning difficulties throughout her school years she pushed through creating her own way forward. At age 22 Sandy was diagnosed as Dyslexic by an optometrist. The prescribed coloured glasses were only a temporary aid and did not address the problem. Her difficulties continued to plague her. Once in the workforce she found her niche in Sales. It made best use of her considerable people skills.

At age 50 she realised the beauty of her abilities and no longer saw her dyslexia as a burden. It truly was a gift. Due to Sandy's personal journey and her battle with learning difficulties, she came to the point of writing a book. The book partly outlines her battle but mostly it is about the empowerment she achieved once she accepted her Dyslexia.

Sandy has decided to take up the fight. Her battle with feeling she was dumb ended the day she decided to see her burden as a gift. Now awakened, she brings her own previously unrecognised gifts

and talents out into the public arena, helping to encourage and motivate others to also accept and embrace their uniqueness.
Sandy has authored 3 books.

- The Old Man at the Coffee Shop. (Fiction)
- Embracing Dyslexia. The chronicles of a personal realisation.
- Releasing the Seven Year Old.
- Currently researching a business book called Mixed Messages.
- Developed a kid's empowerment program called "Patterns"
- Developed an adult's personal empowerment program called "Sense of Self"
- Founder of the "Academy of Young Entrepreneurs Family Renewal Program.
- Has a weekly radio program on YYYFM Community Radio called the Ministry of Buzz.
- Creator of Belief Systems Magazine (BS Mag)

sandy@embracingdyslexia.com.au
www.embracingdyslexia.com.au
...and much more.

How yoga and meditation helped me overcome grief

In March 2014, my husband and I lost our baby 21 weeks into the pregnancy. She was a miracle, as we had been told we would not be able to conceive. The road to conception had been a challenge every step of the way, with intrusive procedures for us both, little hope of success, multiple hospital visits, reactions to the IVF drugs, intense morning sickness and more. But all of this was bearable when we discovered the procedure had been a success: they had made us a baby and I was pregnant.

My husband joined me at the 20 week scan, having just felt the first kick from our baby, full of excitement to discover if it was a boy or a girl. Instead, we were faced with news that there was no amniotic fluid. This is commonly known in the medical world as PROM (Premature Rupture of Membrane). We were given the option to conservatively manage the pregnancy or terminate then and there.

We chose to manage the pregnancy as in our shock the idea of terminating was beyond us both, but after just a tiny bit of research we knew deep down that it would become the only option. Thankfully nature took its course and the decision was taken out of our hands. Within one week I was septic from infection and she was on her way. There was no hope of a live birth. We were devastated.

I remember the day I gave birth like it was yesterday. My body can still feel every stage, every movement, every contraction. I doubt that will ever change, though I'm glad to say as time goes on it does get easier, lighter. I had to go into surgery directly after birth as the placenta wouldn't come away – it rarely detaches so early in the pregnancy, even with complications.

As I came round from the general anaesthetic I started hallucinating. I was having an allergic reaction to the antibiotics, which on top of the cocktail of drugs I had received in the previous 12 hours, was having a rather strong and lively effect. I remember it vividly: I was observing it almost as an out of body experience. I sat up, halfway between lucid and totally out of it, crying my eyes out, saying over and over, 'it's not right, it's not right'. The nurses thought I meant the loss of my baby girl, but I was talking about the way I felt physically and the mad, shaking visions I was having each time I closed my eyes, seeing all sorts of faces in a kaleidoscope fashion in my head. It was more than I was able to process after the trauma I'd already been through.

The nurses and my consultant were amazing, though, and quickly worked out what was wrong. Once the antibiotics were stopped I soon settled back to normal and was allowed to see my husband again and leave the recovery ward. Exhausted by the night's events and overcome with grief, we were shells of our former selves.

It was now that they gave us the option of meeting our baby. I knew immediately that I wanted to see her. I was scared, but intuition told me it was something that I needed to do, regardless of my fears. I was to stand alone in this action though, as my husband was resolute that he didn't want to meet her.

I am so glad I did. The peace and calm I felt when I held her was like nothing I had ever known before. I felt so utterly whole with her laying in my hands. I didn't know it then, but this little girl, this baby who had never lived in this world, would end up being the most profound teacher I have ever had. The moments with her gave me strength to feel that everything could be OK. That we would get through this pain and sadness.

But with no backup embryos at the hospital and therefore no hope of future attempts, my husband couldn't see a path back to happiness. During a time when I needed him the most he was putting an increasing amount of distance between us. His reasoning was that I would not be happy without a baby and that I deserved a chance to have a family. I reassured him over and over that I would choose him over a baby and family any day and that I was not going to give up on us. Almost 10 years of marriage and over 13 years together was far more important to me and I was ready to fight for it.

I learnt a great deal during that time, realising that different people deal with grief in so many different ways. Where my husband and I were concerned, we were, unfortunately, at polar opposites. I wanted to meet our baby, hold her, have a funeral, name her, sob my heart out, grieve her loss, talk about it, lean on family, friends, colleagues and take time to let it settle. My husband preferred to get on as normal, not really giving any time and space to the vast happening in our lives – not ignoring it, but careful not to dwell on it and certainly not sharing it with others, including me. I could see we were approaching it differently, but regardless of this, throughout the grieving period I tried so hard to make him see how much I loved him. I tried to get us to a counsellor, but my attempts only distanced him further and his communication fell away almost entirely. Finally he was able to tell me: he was going to call it a day. We were over.

The day he left I almost broke. I have never known such grief was possible. I have never cried so much in my life. I remember sobbing down the phone to my mum, barely able to breath between the tears. I was already broken-hearted by the loss of our baby girl, still recovering physically as well as emotionally – but this eclipsed everything I felt for her. Losing him was beyond imaginable. He was my world. I was going to grow old with him, with or without babies, and right then I needed him.

Each moment I looked to the future I was filled with fear. How would I exist without him? What would my future be without the security of the home we had just bought, without his family who I love deeply, without everything I thought to be me? I was losing my identity. Living was not something that appealed and the fear that came with it took over my entire body. My interest in food was lost, it was like eating stones. I lost weight, my skin was dull, my eyes puffy. I developed IBS and couldn't go near caffeine as it increased the shakes I already had and aggravated my insides. I was a wreck.

However, in the moments between sobbing – the heart wrenching, noisy, physical kind of sobbing that leaves you without, clears you of everything within – I managed to realise I had a choice. Break or pick myself up. With immeasurable support and help from my close family and friends I managed to choose the latter and I picked myself up. Their love and support gave me something to be grateful for even when I felt I had lost everything. With no faith in the universe and its power to guide me on the right path, I was at least able to find gratitude for them.

One particular friend is a yoga teacher. She had recently run the London Marathon and as part of her fundraising she ran a raffle, with the top prize being a private lesson with her. I won. It was perfect timing, like the universe was starting to take care of me again – not that I really saw this at the time, I was still clouded by grief, but it was a glimmer of something good at least. We waited till I was physically improved and then, with her close guidance, I began to learn yoga – and with it, the ability to control my anxiety, pain, sadness and fear.

With each lesson I felt a new sense of calm and lightness. Simply learning to breathe again brought balance back to my body. My life had been turned upside down and shaken out, yet she was able to ground me. And with my feet planted firmly in each day I found a way to move forward, minutes at first, then hours, then whole days. Slowly I began to realise that today was just a tiny bit better than yesterday and in fact a great deal better than last week – so that even if today was a bit flat, the improvement from sobbing my way through a whole day was vast. I no longer wished for a bus to knock me down simply to find peace. I was finding that peace through the daily practice of yoga.

With the encouragement of another dear friend I let this lack of care for my life liberate me and decided to do a sky dive. It was something I had always wanted to do, but I had always been too afraid as my life was 'too good': I had felt I had too much to lose. Now was the perfect time. The experience gave me a brief break from the intense anxiety I was feeling and turned the negative fear into something truly positive. When my feet touched the ground I wanted to get right back in that plane and do it all over again. I had a grin on my face and a spring in my step for a few precious moments. I felt in control.

Invigorated by the jump, my friend and I started to plan. This was a chance to take the sorrow and despair and turn it into something positive. To remove myself from the path my ex-husband and circumstance had placed me on and carve out a new one. A chance to change my life entirely and to step away from the confines I had built around me over the years. I had lost all that I thought underpinned my identity. I needed to discover who I was again. So I quit my job and left for Africa on a trip of a lifetime: coast to coast in 56 days, with some time in Cape Town at the end.

I walked with lions, held snakes, rode elephants, camped with hyenas, climbed enormous rocks, walked to the edge and drank it all in. I threw myself out of another plane, jumped off a gorge, quad biked, ate, drank and was merry! I was alive again. If someone had told me this two months beforehand, I would never have believed them.

Throughout the trip I continued to practice yoga to help control any negative thoughts or emotions. By the end of the trip I was pretty happy and in a good place. Living day to day without dwelling on the past or worrying about the future, feet planted firmly in today, I managed to find peace within myself. I had found acceptance of what happened and stopped the endless questions of 'why?' and the pointless wishing for things to be different. I left broken and came back healed. Of course, the space and vast landscapes helped — I truly learned to breathe in Africa — but most of all I think the time away from London and my 'normal' everyday life gave me the opportunity to search within myself for the balance that I had lost.

That, and I managed to fall just-the-right-amount in love with a beautiful young Canadian guy who opened up my heart again to the possibility of love with someone else. I was no longer invisible — as I felt I had been to my husband for so long. It felt good to find beauty in another man, and to be desired again. He was perfectly timed, and a complete surprise — for a long time I had truly believed I could never love another man, or be loved in return.

During my last few weeks in Africa, not feeling ready to be back 'home' just yet, I started to formulate a plan for continuing my travel before settling into a new life. I had come to realise that though I lost a great deal that year, I had also been given a gift. Time in my life with no responsibilities, no attachments, no partner, no job. It seemed I had to make the most of it before tying myself into a new everyday pattern, once again filled with constraints and limitations.

I read a book about Burmese elephants called Elephant Moon by John Sweeney and became excited by the idea of seeing them. So began the hatching of a new plan. The young Canadian man I had fallen just-the-right-amount in love with convinced me that Nepal was a must-see place, and that the Everest trek was out of this world. With that in mind, seeing as they were just next door I decided to visit Thailand and Vietnam as well. And India: with the benefits I was feeling through my yoga practice, the idea of spending time at an ashram really began to appeal to me.

All of a sudden the universe started speaking to me again, sending people along the way to guide me. People I met in bars and restaurants, gifts of Guru photos and recommendations — so many people seemed to be pointing me in that direction.

Getting back to London in December was full of challenges. The ongoing and arduous sale of our home threatened my financial ability to travel, while my ex-husband's new relationship brought renewed emotional turmoil – just as we were beginning divorce proceedings. Although I was leaps and bounds on from where I had been before my trip, I took large steps back and discovered my new sense of calm was not quite as secure as I might have thought!

I found I was still struggling with the idea of wanting my ex-husband to think well of me. His opinion was still important to me. I asked for a dinner date so that we could catch up and I could share with him all my experiences and show him how well I was doing. A moment to be friends and people with one another rather than ex-spouses only dealing with legalities. He agreed and I looked forward to it.

Then he cancelled. There followed a month of him making and cancelling dates for various reasons. By the time we finally met, the dinner has lost its meaning: I was as close to angry as I ever got in the whole process, and certainly disappointed with what I took to be his disregard for my **feelings.**

As my Vipassana teacher would later tell me, 'In any situation I ask myself: What happiness will come of this?' The month was an incredible learning curve, and while I continued to care for my ex-husband I began to realise that I didn't need him in my life any more, that I would be OK without him. If we could manage to be friends it would be nice, but for now that wasn't a possibility. Besides, I had so many wonderful friends on hand that not having his friendship was no longer such an issue. A weight lifted and I no longer worried about his opinion of me

On Christmas Eve morning, after a month of thinking we would lose our buyer for the flat and when it looked like I would have to drop the dream of more travel and spiritual development, I finally got the good news that we had exchanged. Travel to South East Asia and the 'discovery' part of my journey was given the green light. It was the best Christmas present in the world! My family was all there and with bubbles, lots of smiles, hugs and a few tears I thanked them for their amazing support in getting me to that day.

Then came a second Christmas miracle. My ex-husband had clearly spent some time thinking over the holiday period (our first Christmas apart in 13 years). Just a couple of days ahead of New Years' Eve, he sent me an email, apologising for the way he had handled the whole situation and his lack of communication regarding his feelings throughout the process. It was so unexpected and so wonderful to receive: having this apology was more than I had hoped would ever happen. It also confirmed my faith that he was a good man who had lost his way and who was slowly making his way back. It provided incredible closure.

So began 2015 and planning! Research, flights, shopping, visas and jabs. It wasn't easy finding an ashram – with next to no knowledge I was at the mercy of Google – but one particular ashram stood out: the Sivananda Yoga Vedanta Dhanwantari Ashram in Kerala. After discovering a close girlfriend of mine had actually been there, I decided it was the place for me.

The director of the ashram persuaded me that the best course of action was a one month intense Teacher Training Course. It took me a long time to decide, due to not really wanting to become a teacher as well as the cost of the course. But I think I knew all along that it was the right direction for me. It was the best decision I had made in a long time.

It's hard to put into words what I learnt there, but it blew my mind and gave me such strength. I met wonderful people, both there and on my way there. Most importantly, I finally left my sadness behind and discovered that my story was no longer my identity. I found my smile again, a true smile, the kind of grin that has no control and doesn't care how it looks, open and beaming. What's more, having uhm'd and ahh'd for months, I decided to go back to my maiden name. I felt great when I received my Teacher Training certificate and saw the name Tara Scammell in bold letters, slap bang in the middle.

Positively glowing, sparking, floating and generally high on how good life can be I headed to the Himalayas for some serious trekking (a prospect that would have been unthinkable six months earlier). Unable to decide between Annapurna and Everest I decided to do both: Annapurna Base Camp first and then Everest Base Camp after a couple of days' rest in Kathmandu. The trekking and the mountains gave me the time and space to let all the teachings of the past month settle and permeate their way through. I found such clarity in the mountains, observing my inner self, and started to realise things, even have new ideas.

I celebrated the anniversary of my baby girl, Isla May, at Annapurna Base Camp. It was by coincidence that we ended up there that day, but it couldn't have been more perfect. I spent the day trekking to the top with some wonderful people I met along the way and, most importantly, with a smile on my face. I didn't cry that day. I found gratitude: for everything Isla taught me and for my ex-husband for having the courage to leave. I never thought I would be able to feel truly happy for losing Isla – I thought I would carry the weight of her loss with me forever and simply learn to live with it – but there it was, clear as day and free as a bird. I felt that not being where I was at that moment, and being with my ex-husband instead, was truly unimaginable. When I got back to Kathmandu I messaged him and thanked him. I was released.

Although I didn't go the ashram to become a teacher, as I continued on my journey I found myself teaching more and more. This happened in many different ways: some obvious, with people wanting to join my 5am yoga practice, or teach them how to do a headstand, but also in more subtle ways. Discussions would start and I would talk about what I had been doing, sometimes with a full in depth story and other times with barely a detail. Either way, I found many people were inspired by either my story or me.

It was surprising at first. I honestly don't think my story is any different from the next: so many people have gone through the same, and much worse, and have still come out smiling. But something seemed to inspire a reaction in people. I felt that I was like a mirror reflecting something back to people that they had forgotten was inside themselves: a desire for a more spiritual, inward perspective, or for a clearer and simpler way of life.

As I continued my journey though Nepal, I was struck by the spiritual nature of the people there. They are so kind and open, so giving, that if they have nothing they will be sure to give you 100% of their nothing, share it with you willingly and take great joy in your acceptance and pleasure. I was welcomed into so many homes along the way and treated like royalty.

They also have such a strong spiritual practice: up before the crack of dawn making offerings, lighting incense, going to the temple – all before the day's work begins. I was inspired by their dedication and found great joy in waking super early, walking the steps to the great stupa in Monkey Temple and sitting with three Buddhist Monks in a small meditation room just off the hustle and bustle of the main temple, followed by a full yoga session on the rooftop of my backpackers and finally a hearty breakfast.

I was sad to leave Kathmandu after a month in Nepal, but it was time to have some new experiences and see if I would apply my new practices away from the support of the wonderful people I had met there.

Then onto Myanmar and the temples! 'My name is Tara Scammell and I am addicted to temples.'

I had begun learning to meditate at the ashram, and continued to practice walking meditation in Nepal, but it was all very new and if I'm honest I wasn't very good at it. Fidgety, uncomfortable, thinking at a million miles an hour the moment someone told me to stop thinking. Barely managing 10 minutes of physical stillness, let alone any level of mental calm. It was definitely not my forte. As it turns out, it's not really anyone's forte at first! But it's well worth sticking with it, as I later discovered...

In Myanmar, I got the chance to start sitting with Buddha. It wasn't easy at first: I felt a lot of resistance and aversion to many of the Buddhist practices, much as I do with any religion. But once I got over them and started simply sitting with Buddha, I found I liked him more and more. I wasn't learning about his teachings, just finding peace in his presence. Taking it all at my own pace. I was realizing that I could find peace in any chaotic situation, of which there are many in South East Asia. It dawned on me that it wasn't the situation that gave me peace at all, rather myself.

At the end of Myanmar I remembered hearing of a retreat from someone at the Sivananda ashram. It was a meditation retreat at a monastery in Thailand where you are silent for 10 days. At the time I'd felt it was probably beyond me: my meditation was very weak and the idea of doing it all day, every day, without discussion, was too much. It stayed with me, though, and despite my flights conflicting with the dates of the retreat I found I was drawn to it. It was a first come, first served retreat with no booking system and I liked that idea. If it was meant to be then it would happen. So I took the plunge and changed my flight to see what would happen.

It was the next best decision I'd made! I learnt so much at Wat Kow Tham, even learnt that much of what I was already doing was in the Buddha's teachings. Now I have a format and structure to link them to and improve how they help me. I realised a great deal about myself, including my self-doubt which, despite my confident demeanour, is far stronger than I have ever acknowledged.

Most importantly, though, after weeks of wanting so much to find true forgiveness for my ex-husband, I finally found it. I learnt loving kindness meditation and directed it at him for 8 days. As soon as I learnt to let go of 'what he did', to stop engaging in his past actions and my past pain, once I started seeing him as a suffering human being just the same as me, it was easy. Instead of identifying with the past I created space around the thought through wisdom. In doing so, there was nothing for that thought to hold onto anymore and it simply fell away.

I emailed my ex-husband actually saying the words 'I forgive you' and wished him joy and peace in his lifes. The joy and lightness I now have encourages me to continue down this path.

Looking back on the events of the past year, I've come to realise the importance of opening up to others about life's difficulties. I am a very open person and always have been, and I was happy to talk freely about everything that happened last year; it saved me. Right from the start I had been open about the IVF treatment, so lots of our friends and family had followed our journey through the process. I found the support we gained from this incredibly helpful during a testing time in my life.

When we had finally accepted the pregnancy was happening, we announced on Facebook (as you do) that we were expecting a baby. The response was immense, as so many of our friends and family knew the troubles we had been having. I remember such joy in those moments, sharing the good news with so many people who had wished it would happen for us. Later, in my grief, I found the courage to use Facebook to communicate our loss with those people who cared about me.

I announced we had lost Isla, that she had arrived too early for this world, and the response I received was astonishing. So much love and support from all corners of the world. More interesting, though, was the response I got from those who had also experienced such loss and those who were trying without hope through countless IVF rounds and treatment.

It seems that infertility and child loss is somewhat of a taboo topic in the UK. We see it as something shameful, something to hide and not talk about in public. So when I opened up to this in a public forum I heard privately from a number of my friends, some of whom I had not realised were going through a similar painful and hopeless journey. Even in my darkest moments I found I was connecting with people, helping them by opening the channels of communication on such a painful topic. It was so healing to be able to help others even at that early stage when I felt all I was doing was leaning on anyone who could support me.

I remember something a close friend said to me one day. I had just mentioned how lucky I was to have such wonderful caring and supportive friends. Her response was to say, 'It's not luck Tara. You have wonderful friends because you have been a wonderful friend. It takes time and effort to develop and nurture such friendships, not luck.' I liked her sentiment and at a time when I was taking a great deal from my friends it was of some comfort to realise that it was perfectly acceptable and simply my time to take for a while.

Now all those same people have been watching my journey remotely as I travel both physically and spiritually. I know they are with me, sending me love and support as I discover my new path in life. Even better, I can send that love and support right back to them, encouraging them to lose the fear we build up in our lives, be brave and make those changes you were thinking about. Breathe and improve your appreciation of the present moment.

Now I'm sat in a wonderful café in Vietnam, The Hanoi Social Club, writing this. I'm in my final country on this part of my journey and I find myself, yet again, not planning to go back to 'normal' life just yet. Perhaps never. I am too far down this path of discovery to turn back right now. There is too much to be learnt and discovered and I have big ideas that I can only put into action with more learning.

So though I'm not sad about going home, as I will love seeing everyone, I do find myself planning a little for the next stage. Perhaps off to India for three months of Karma Yoga and a chance to sharpen my teaching skills. More certainly, though, back to the monastery to volunteer there, spend time learning more from the Buddha's teachings and deepen my practice with hope for true insight. Vipassana means clear sight, and I certainly have that right now.

Tara Scammell

About the author

Originally destined for the stage, Tara Scammell trained in the performing arts from a young age, but as a teenager decided her place was behind the camera in production.

At 18 she headed to London and started her career in Music TV Production working with artists from The Beatles and Kate Bush to Justin Timberlake and AVICCI.

Never quite giving up on the performance side of things she has been a member of the Crouch End Festival Chorus, one of London's best symphonic choirs, for over 12 years. During that time she has performed and recorded with artists such as Andrea Bocelli, Enio Morricone, Goldfrapp & Noel Gallagher in London, on tour and in festivals such as Glastonbury.

After life changing events last year she has spent the past year travelling the globe and stripping back her life on an exploration of her inner self, in search of a happier existence.

Now a qualified yoga teacher, Tara is considering a new project - in which she can work with young people through yoga and meditation to help them deal with issues around confidence, anxiety, self-belief and acceptance.

STAY AHEAD OF THE GAME

NEXT GEN TRADER.COM

Why I became an organ donor

I can't quite remember when the thought of becoming an organ donor first entered my mind. I do remember as a young child my mum and dad had a plaque hanging on the wall that said "do unto others as you would have others do unto you." The golden rule, it was called, now the plaque hangs proudly in my home. I've always had that sense of oneness, of being a part of something bigger than me, the sense that we are all one, that we are all connected. I remember as a child, wanting to be remembered as someone who made a difference, who is generous. This is for the most part how I have aspired to live my life.

Thinking back, it was about 10 years ago when I first considered organ donation. I learned of people giving their kidneys to family members and thinking I would be willing to do that for someone. I remember being in a Business Network Group, and sitting with one of my friends in that group and she was telling me how she was preparing to donate her kidney to her brother. I thought, wow, that's so special. I remember talking to my wife about the idea of donating my kidney, and initially her thoughts were that it was too dangerous and risky and she really didn't want me to do it, so I put the idea on the backburner.

I found out not long after that my friend in the business group, actually had the opportunity to donate her kidney to her brother and created a better life for him. Seeing what a difference my friend made brought the idea of donating a kidney back again in my mind.

I thought, wouldn't that be awesome to be able to do that! But each time, I brought it up with my family it was met with fear, it was definitely not out of selfishness, but just out of fear for me and my health, so once again it was put on the backburner. I learned that my sister in law's sister, (my brother's wife's sister) donated her kidney for their brother and literally saved his life by doing that, and she was fine, perfectly healthy and living a normal life. I raised the idea of donating my kidney again and once more, it was put aside due to concerns for my health and for my family, if something went wrong.

Defining Moments

Then a few years later, a friend of mine, the son of a very dear friend, passed away. He was only 25 years old and he died of a brain tumor, which was very, very sad.

This was a pivotal moment, a paradigm shift occurred for me at this point.

I remember at that point of my life, I wished there was something I could have done for Josh, but I guess there was nothing I could have done for him. Then back in 2010, another friend of mine passed away due to cancer, and I can remember the anguish, the pain, that his family went through as they were going through the process with him. He was such a fit, strong young man that you didn't think anything could defeat him. Initially, he beat the cancer and went into remission. Before he was diagnosed, he was about 110 kilos, he was a body builder and the cancer stripped him down to about 70kilos. As he recovered, he went back to 95 kgs, and we all thought that he had it beaten. It was in the January of 2010 that it came back and it came back with a vengeance. He became sick quickly, and it got into his liver and at that point, I thought that's it. My next thought was you know maybe, just maybe there's a chance I can give him a part of my liver to help him recover. We inquired about whether it was possible, we were basically told that with this kind of cancer, that's not an option, and I was told that because I wasn't a family member, I couldn't do it. Basically within days Craig passed away, which was very, very difficult for me to accept. However, it was at that point I said, I'm going to do something now, I have thought about this for too long, there was nothing I could have done to help Craig with his cancer, but there's somebody out there that's unwell, not having a very good quality of life, and I could give them one of my kidneys and they could lead a great life.

I started making inquiries, I rang the local renal unit up here in Queensland where I live, and was basically told that, for non-family members, it's illegal. They did tell me that they thought it's legal somewhere in Western Australia so I made inquiries and nobody actually got back to me. I just continued my investigations.

I actually managed to get the attention of "The Sunrise show" (this is an Australian daily breakfast show) to see, if in some way they could help me to find a way that this can be done. It was through the Sunrise show that I connected with a Renal Physician from Sydney where she said it is permissible to do an altruistic donation, and it was from that moment the journey started for me. The next 6 months, were taken up with physical examinations, physical tests and psychological evaluations, because they wanted to know why I was wanting to do this and that it was for the right reasons and that there was no ulterior motive behind what I was doing. It was a very, very interesting process to go through that. The great thing was, it was through that test that I found physically I was in great shape, which made my wife Karen very happy. I got the whole psychological test to prove that I wasn't insane. My family still didn't understand why I wanted to donate my kidney, but Karen certainly gave me her full support.

It took a few years to actually get to the point of the transplant coming to fruition. As I was a living donor, they gave me the opportunity to make sure the recipient was going to be the best possible match for my kidney. There were a couple of false starts - one of the recipients that they had identified, before we could get ourselves organized for the operation, found a deceased donor that was a match, which was great. There was another one that we were getting organized to do the transplant for, and they became too ill, and couldn't, the doctors didn't think that they were strong enough to survive the operation. But eventually, there was a match that the doctors believed was perfect, we organized the date, and we had 6 weeks to prepare. I went to Sydney, and my doctor, gave me all the information I needed to know. For me, it was something that I really, really wanted to do, so I was looking forward to it. We were admitted to the hospital, the doctor was very kind, and as Karen and I were finished having a family, he agreed to give me a vasectomy while he was in there, which was also meant I wouldn't have to go through the discomfort of another operation. I can remember that morning we went into hospital, for me it was very, very exciting to be going through the process, getting dressed in the gowns, getting into the little bed and waiting for the doctors and nurses to take me from one area of the hospital to the next. A young resident doctor came in and she asked if she could do a story on me for university. She said she would be there throughout the operation and she would also be there when they put the kidney in the recipient. I was put under anesthetic and the next minute I was waking up and it was all over. From everyone's point of view it was a total success, the young doctor came back and visited me and she was so excited she said that in the moment that my kidney was attached to the blood vessels in the recipients body it was instant and there was no problem whatsoever it was working properly and it was so fantastic, this was the first time in many, many years that the body on its own could filter the blood. I was feeling uplifted and fulfilled, it was the most rewarding thing for me that I have ever done in my life - that I was able to help somebody. In the next four days I recovered in hospital.

On Saturday it was time to go home so I left from hospital and we caught our flight and we were home on that Saturday. I remembered that was Saturday lunch time when I got a pain in my stomach, it was like gas pains but the worst gas pains I'd ever experienced. For the rest of afternoon I was wondering how I can get rid of this gas in my belly and feeling a little bit kind of silly and wimpy. It was about 2 o'clock in the morning when I couldn't take the pain any longer so we went down to the hospital and explained what was going on. They tried a few things which didn't work so they admitted me to the hospital on that Sunday morning. A Doctor came and saw me and examined me, he really couldn't find anything, his thought was though that as the kidney was removed through access via key-hole surgery, and that the movement and disruption of the bowel can cause some issues.

So I went through Sunday and nothing really changed I still had the pains. On Monday, it was still the same and I decided to try and eat, I didn't feel like eating but they gave me a quarter of a big meal to eat, and it was very painful. Monday was still the same and when I woke up Tuesday morning and everything was still the same, I didn't think it was quite right. At around lunch time on the Tuesday I had never felt quite so unwell and started to vomit up everything I ate the day before, it all came out and the doctors came in. They asked me to relax so they could get a tube through my nose into my stomach - damn it was disgusting! Eventually I got it down. Then they gave me this fluid to drink which shows up on X-ray. They could see that the fluid got to a certain point within my intestine and stopped so they realized that there was an obstruction.

The Doctor said I had to go back in to surgery which I wasn't excited about. The initial surgery I had to remove the kidney was very small (key hole surgery) and this time, they had to open up my stomach, so it was more vanity than anything else I didn't really want to have a big scar going up my belly. I went into surgery about 7pm and I think we got out about 11:30, I remember just waking up for a moment, they gave me stuff to sleep and pain killers. I woke up the next morning and the doctor came in and told me that if they hadn't gone back in last night it could have been very, very serious, I could have been knocking on heaven's door which shook us a little bit. He explained that it was a very rare thing to happen, when they remove the kidney they have to move the bowels out of the way.

There is a lining around the bowels which must have been nicked slightly by the surgeon removing my kidney and when everything went back in place a small bit of my small intestine went through a little hole in that wall and twisted onto itself which is the obstruction. Basically what the doctor had to do was pull out everything, repair the wall and put everything back. What he was concerned about was the portion of intestine had been strangulated for so long, he was not sure that it would revive; he contemplated removing that section of intestine. If he had done that it would have been far worse for me as I would have had to wear one of those colostomy bags on the outside of me. I went right through to the next Sunday, not eating. I am not a heavy person and when I went into the hospital in Sydney, I was 80 kilos and by this time now I was down about 68 kilos which meant I lost about 12 kilos which is a lot of weight for me. By that Monday the doctor said that if something doesn't happen soon, they may have to operate again and remove that section of intestine, he gave it one more day. I passed wind for the first time in over 2 weeks that Tuesday morning, the nurses were so excited, and we were all excited. The doctor said it was the first time and probably the last time in your life that people will cheer and celebrate when you pass wind.

From that moment on my body went into recovery mode, and life started returning to normal. Basically for a couple of weeks I was still a little bit tender after having holes in my stomach opened up. The pain and complication that happened is not something I think about daily, what I do think about daily is, if I had the opportunity to do it again, I would, as it was just a great rewarding feeling. I never actually met the recipient, I didn't know whether they were young or old or male or female, under the guidelines and rules of the altruistic donation the two parties are not allowed to meet. A few weeks after I got home, the transplant unit in Sydney sent me a card which the recipient passed on saying that for the last 5 years they had been on dialysis which didn't give them a good quality of life. There were so many things they couldn't do with their family but now it was like a new life for them, which was awesome. The complication just doesn't mean a thing, it was all worth it and I would gladly do it again.

Since going through that experience, what it did bring home to me was the number of people that are actually on an organ donation waiting lists, waiting for a transplant. There's some 2000 people on the waiting list right now in Australia, two people die every week waiting for the call that they found someone who is a match. It shouldn't be 2000 people, what we need is more people not necessarily doing what I'm doing, not being a living donor, but just someone who puts their hand up, who will say that if they pass away, if their organs are healthy, they would like to have their organs save the life of others. My mission is to get that word out, to spread the word of becoming an organ donor, to encourage people to have a discussion with their family, because there's a rule in Australia that if your family, upon your passing, decides not to donate your organs, it doesn't make any difference what your wishes were, it doesn't matter. It's up to them whether you're allowed to help other people in your death. So for me what I want to do now is help the organization Transplant Australia that has been great to me during pre and post operation. Working with them, I want to help spread that word. What we've been doing in recent years since the operation is focusing on young children (both those who received a transplant and those waiting). We're looking to run some more events around awareness, so we can get people to understand how important organ donation is and what they need to do. As a private pilot, my pilot buddies and I, as our first event, arranged an awareness flight to Horn Island in the Torres Straight and stopped along the way up the Queensland Coast and spread the word. The next event was to gather kids from regional NSW and we flew them out to Dubbo Zoo for a sleepover with the animals, it was an awesome time, follow this link and you will gain an insight into the lives of some these kids and their families. https://www.youtube.com/watch?v=ojkKV_nbeRU&feature=youtu.be

I guess it's a difficult thing to share with someone if you never gone through it but for them they were able to share their stories with us while we were on that great adventure. We are in the middle of planning our next little adventure which will bring some kids up here to the Gold Coast, where they will be able to enjoy the fun and adventure of Sea World and Movie World.

Sea World and the Nara Resort have kindly offered us special rates for accommodation and free entry into both theme parks.

The big challenge for me I guess is getting people to help spread the message. I feel at times uncomfortable talking about what I did because it's sounds a bit like bragging, although if it helps me to get some attention to the situation that so many people are on the waiting list and so many people are dying. That's truly my focus that's what I want to achieve. What we are really looking for is some exposure to have a platform to tell people what's going on and what's possible and how rewarding it can be.

It's a sad thing when someone passes but in the last couple of years, there is a service that is held by Transplant Australia and Donate Life, it's a thanksgiving service where families of deceased donors attend, families of recipients attend and they get to share their stories. It is great to see the joy the families receive knowing that by allowing their loved ones organs to be donated they have saved another one's life -it gave some meaning to it. I'm sure if everyone could understand that, there would be no hesitation. The problem is that if we don't speak to our loved ones about it, in that moment of grief, it's too hard of a decision for them to make. I know in many cases, people look back and think that "if I would have been thinking more clearly, I would have given permission for my loved ones organs to be donated". Because up to 10 people could be saved through the donation of one person that passes away. So the message is, have a chat with your family, let them know that this is something you want to do so they are prepared, so in your passing you can give someone else a chance at life.

Gordon Rutty

About the author

Born 4th November 1963 in Kingston Jamaica.

I am the youngest son to my wonderful parents who through example have taught me what I believe to be great values.

In 1974 my family moved to Australia from Jamaica. The decision was made as my dad wanted a better life us. Jamaica was becoming a very dangerous place to live.

I was a very active kid and loved adventure, whilst I did ok at school I couldn't wait for the weekends to ride motor bikes or just generally be outdoors. I left school after the first semester of grade 12 and joined the work force.

Ambition and a desire to be able to help others has driven me to crave success.

Working hard and going the extra mile are important to me.

Karen and I have recently celebrated 18 years of marriage and we have three great children, Connor 17, Hunter 14, and Lucas 11. My beautiful daughter Georgia 23 from my first marriage lives in Coffs Harbour.

Serving and helping my fellow human beings does not need big sacrifice, one of the things I do is regularly donate blood, this can save many lives.

My potential messages

No matter who you are, you can make a difference, you can have a positive effect on other people lives. Each day it is just a matter of deciding that when you meet someone you want them to better for having met you.

We don't have to be Nelson Mandela's we just need a heart for others and we can have a huge impact.

The Power of Gratitude

Ever since I was a little girl I always wondered what I would be like when I grew up. Now that I'm grown up, I wonder what the rest of my life will be like. You see, we never know what tomorrow can bring; what adventure, what surprise, what mystery will unfold tomorrow no one knows and that is what makes life so amazing.

"Yesterday is history; tomorrow a mystery."
Today is a gift – that is why it is called "the Present,"

As children, it seemed like Christmas was never going to arrive and that the time between school holidays was an eternity. As an adult, I seem to be packing down the Christmas tree when it is time to set up again. Is it just me? Or is time absolutely flying by the older you get?

I spent many years working in the personal development seminar industry and learnt from many great speakers, and I feel that it is my gift to share that knowledge with you. Gifts are all around us, even the challenges that life throws at us can be looked at as gifts if we look hard enough, even though many things don't seem like gifts at all.

In the 37 years I have been on this planet, I have had many truly amazing days. I have also had many days when I just did not want to get out of bed in the morning. We all have those days.

If only it could be Sunday morning every day, when the alarm clock didn't go off, when I don't have to fight traffic, when I don't need to be around other people and I can just stay in my own little world in bed with nothing but beautiful dreams to entertain me all day long.

For the last seven years I have wanted to have more doona days than I have ever had before, that is because seven years ago I was diagnosed with a rare brain disease called Intracranial Hypertension, or IH for short. This is a condition that has no cause and no cure yet! My brain makes too much spinal fluid that puts pressure on my brain, and causes daily headaches that often turn into migraines.

Having a headache 24/7 at times is unbearable. Imagine waking up with the worst hangover you've ever had, knowing that you are going to feel like this all day, all week, all month, all year and for many years to come, until they find a cure.

Before I had surgery and had a VP shunt inserted in my brain, the only relief I got from the feeling that my head is being squished in a vice, was having regular lumbar punctures, which means a 15cm needle is inserted into my spine to drain out the excess spinal fluid. The only problem with this is that it is extremely painful, and if they take out too much fluid, I suffer from a low-pressure headache (which is just as bad, if not worse, than having a high-pressure headache) A low-pressure headache feels like your brain has been sucked dry of all the fluids and it feels like it is caving in (instead of feeling like it's going to explode as it does when I have a high-pressure headache). The more I have, the more dangerous it gets as well, as I have a build-up of scar tissue on my spinal cord making each one even harder to perform. So far I'm up to #30 ☹ ...

I'm not telling you this to get sympathy and to make you to think "Poor Nikki! That's so terrible". I'm sharing this with you so that I can share with you my strength, my courage, my passion and my gratitude.

I could sit in the corner and cry "Poor me! Why did this have to happen to me? Life just isn't fair", but that wouldn't get me anywhere. The crying and the stress only make my headaches worse.

I tell you this so that you will get off your ass and stop your whining about the little things in your life that seems so insignificant when you see the things I have seen. I am here to motivate and inspire you to live your most amazing life possible.

I am here to be your wake-up call to be grateful for everything in your life.

To be grateful for everything you DO have in your life, but so that you are also grateful for all the things that you DO NOT have in your life.

Yes, this is a really crappy condition. When I was diagnosed with it, to tell you I was pissed off would be an understatement, but I have found my gift. I believe I have been given Intracranial Hypertension (IH) so that I can use my voice to raise awareness to help find a cure. You see those with IH suffer in silence. It is what we call a "silent disease." From the outside, some days we look perfectly healthy. We put on a brave face, we work, we play sports (when we are feeling ok), we live our lives, we look after families, just like everybody else. Except, we suffer in chronic pain on a daily basis. When we have high pressure, we would like to hide away from the world and stay at home, tuck ourselves into bed, and dose ourselves up on painkillers to sleep the pain away. If we are lucky to get to sleep, we usually wake up a few hours later still with a high-pressure headache.

Some days are better than others, and we can hide our pain really well. Other days, it's very easy to see how much pain we are in, our eyes squint from any bright lights, they are glassy and hazed over from the pain killers and we have brain fog from too much pressure and trying to balance taking enough pain meds to reduce the pain but not to too much that we can't function.

Having IH is really crappy and I would not wish it on anyone and I am extremely grateful that this is all I have.

Since September 2008 I have had six brain surgeries, 30 lumber punctures, seven MRI scans, over 100 CT scans, over 150 x-rays, a cranial angiogram (that really hurt☹), hundreds of blood tests; you name it, they tested me for it.

After 12 months of having Lumbar punctures every 3-4 weeks to drain off the excess fluid and the medication Diamox giving me really bad side effects, my Neurologist decided that it was time to start talking surgery and referred me to a neurosurgeon, I remember that first conversation was all a bit hazy when he was explaining how they would drill a hole into my skull and insert a tube into the ventricles in my brain and channel a tube down into the peritoneal cavity (the area in your belly all your organs sit in)

It is a really scary thought having brain surgery knowing that my life is in the hands of someone else, I've often thought what if my surgeon sneezed while he had a scalpel inside my brain or drilled too far? I trust him but accidents happen and there are no guarantees in life especially with brain surgery.

So after every surgery when I wake up and I'm in recovery in that drug induced haze and confusion my eyes always glaze over as tears of gratitude roll down my checks as I wiggle my fingers and toes and do my comprehension tests (where are you? What is your name? What did you just have done? Etc)

The tears are sweet relief that the worse is over and its only going to get better from now on, now it is up to me to focus on healing myself and not allowing anything negative into my life. I surround myself in a golden orb I call it my healing bubble and I block out everything else that is going on and just focus on me. Once I get back to the ward I spend almost 24/7 listening to Karen Drucker healing and meditation music to block out the negative and disruptive noises of the hospital. Her songs are all about self-love, healing, love and Gratitude. She really is AMAZING ....

It has been an interesting journey over the last few years and one I wish I myself and others did not have to go through, but it has shaped and moulded me into who I am today.

Even though I've had a lot of pain & heartache in my life, I feel my life is truly blessed and I am grateful everyday for everything I do have and everything I don't have. Life could be so much worse! We live in such a lucky country.

I have the most amazing bed with clean sheets a feather doona, feather pillows; I have a warm shower every day with clean fresh fluffy towels. I have an amazing wardrobe with many clothes (in fact, too many clothes to choose from). I have over 60 pairs of shoes (okay, I have a fetish, I know). I can get in my car and drive where ever I want to, I can drink clean water, I have electricity, Iphone, Ipad, Ipod & Macbook, I am able to have beautiful fresh fruit and vegetables daily, have three healthy meals (okay, sometimes not-so-healthy). I had a virtually free education for 12 years of my life, most of my medical bills have been paid by Medicare, (though I have paid over $7,000 in things not covered), I can read and write (with the help of spell checker lol), I have the power to vote, even though there is no one worth voting for; I am grateful for everything.

I am also extremely grateful for the things that I don't have. I'm not afraid that if I walk down the street I could be killed, raped or beaten up because of the colour of my skin, my religion, or "just because I'm female ". I don't have to worry about where my next meal will come from or where I will sleep tonight.

I don't have to eat food out of a rubbish bin or sleep under a bridge. I don't have to pretend that I forgot my glasses because I can't read and write, I don't have to suffer in pain without medication or worse, even die, because I can't afford health insurance. I am not frightened that I live in a war torn country where my house could be bombed, raided or burned down in the middle of the night and even though I don't have much money and most weeks live pay check to pay check I am so much richer than millions of people around the world who live on less than $2 a day, You see there are so many things to be grateful for, for what we do have, but sometimes we forget to be grateful for what we don't have. All you have to do is turn on the world news and see the pain and destruction of our planet – then look at your life and realise that no matter how tough you think your life is I bet there is millions of people in the world who would swap lives with you in a heart beat.

Gratitude has been one of the biggest lessons I have learnt in my life and instead of filling the rest of this chapter telling you how amazing I am;

which I could easily fill a whole book ☺ I decided to share with you the AMAZING LIFE LESSONS that have moulded me into who I am today, so hopefully YOU will be able to learn and grow from reading this and gain the confidence to see how amazing you are as well ☺

* Be Confident and LOVE YOUR BODY!

I'll always be cuddly/curvaceous but I won't let myself get obese again. 18 months ago I was a size 22-24 and now I'm a comfortable size 16, I don't have the bone structure to ever get to a size 6 like some of girlfriends nor do I want to work that hard to look like that, I was not blessed to be naturally thin and have to work hard if I ever want to get smaller than a size 12 and even when I did, when I was 21, I was very bony and looked unhealthy at times and it was so hard to maintain and it was just unrealistic for me to stay that thin (for me anyway – everyone is different) .. The main thing with body image is about you being happy with yourself ... it took years for me to love and except my curves .. You only get one body so worship it... accept it with all its flaws even the super models don't see themselves as perfect so why should you. Have confidence with your body.. Have sex with the light ON ... GO on, I dare you! Let everything jiggle and wobble, he will Love it.. If you think you are sexy your man will think your sexy ... WORK IT GIRL. Confidence is very sexy.

* Don't settle for less than you deserve.

It breaks my heart to see people settling for less than they deserve, whether it is a job they get just to pay the bills or a relationship just so they are not single. Aim high with everything you want to achieve in life! Look for the best job; one that fills your heart with passion, and the relationship that makes you glow.

Know that it is okay to be single until you find Mr or Ms Right. And also know that you can find Mr or Ms Right NOW. That person may not be the one you want to spend the rest of your life with, but he or she may be just what you want and need for the next few months. Just don't get too heart broken when it ends as they were only meant to be here for a reason or a season not a lifetime, Some people are here for a good time not a long time.

Allow yourself to make mistakes, but learn from others when you can. Mistakes are a part of life. We all need to make them but we also need to learn not make them again. IF you do make the same mistake twice, it's okay. Go easy on yourself. Don't beat yourself up, especially if you repeat the same mistake in a relationship. I have made lots of mistakes in my life and so does everyone. No one is perfect, even that person you are thinking of right now, saying, "but.... X... is perfect! They never make mistakes!" Trust me, they do. Mistakes are part of life. Learn to love them, accept them, and grow from them.

But when you do make the same mistake for the second time you need to stop and analyse the situation and your beliefs & actions and work out why you did the same thing twice so that you won't do it a third, ask a trusted advisor or friend for their constructive criticism/help as sometime we have no self awareness to our own behaviour but it is very obvious to those around us.

It is not all about what you know, but how you apply what you know.
This is a "Biggy." I always hear people say, "Oh, I heard this speaker talk before and I know all that." You can hear something a hundred times, but unless you are putting it into action, it does not matter how much you know. It might be the 101st time you hear it that it makes sense to you, or is said in a different way that makes you take action. Once you apply it, then you can say that you know it.

Model your life after people who are producing the results that you want.
I love modelling. I'm not taking about the catwalk modelling. Although I do love taking photos and selfies   lol.. I'm talking about what you were told not to do in school (copy others), looking at people that are successful in the areas that you want to be and model your behaviour after theirs, being aware of the mistakes they have made, you can make your journey a lot easier. You don't always need to take the hard road.

Who are people that you admire and respect?
It could be someone in business who is famous like Sir Richard Branson or it might be the owner of the café down the road that makes every customer feel like family.
You might admire and respect people Oprah or Mother Theresa or all the volunteers that give so selflessly for their charity work. What about relationships?
Do you know people, who are still madly in love on their 50th wedding anniversary?
How do these people so in love, speak to and about their partner, what is the behaviour of a loving devoted spouse?

What about being a great parent?
Who are great mother and father role models in your life?
What are their qualities and values?
How can you apply them to your life?

Whenever I get stuck in a tricky situation that I don't know how to get out of I often think 'what would my mentors do'
 If they were in the same spot how would they handle it?
As sometimes we need to think greater than our own capabilities and push ourselves to think outside the box.

Contributing & giving back fills my heart joy! Being able to give back is the easiest need to fulfil. There are so many ways that this need can be met. You can contribute your time, money, energy or love or a combination of all of the above.
The more you give, the more comes back to you in return. That is the law of reciprocity.
But don't give BECAUSE you will get something in return! Give because you want to give. And anything that the universe gives you is just a bonus!
There are plenty of charity's you can Google to pick one. In Australia, try Everydayhero.com.au. It is a donations site for hundreds of Australian Charities you can pick one and donate. If you are in the US the site is firstgiving.com.
 Are there elderly people in your neighbourhood that might need something done around the house that you could help with? You could mow their lawn or do some weeding or some handy man stuff around the house. Even changing a light bulb could really help if someone is a bit unsteady on their feet and they can't climb a ladder to change the light bulb.
Why not knock on an elderly neighbour's door and let them know that you would like to help them out for the next few hours? Do they have any jobs they need doing? Sometimes, just sitting and chatting is a great way of giving back.
Since 2008, I have been a volunteer on the committee for a charity called "Basket Brigade." They are part of the Magic Moments Foundation started by Tony Robbins. We pack and deliver Christmas hampers for the poor and needy every year. This gives me so much joy knowing that I am helping change the lives of families that are struggling at Xmas time, Every year we ask businesses and people in the community to donate cash, food, toiletries, toys, gifts and just about anything they think a family in need might need or want at Christmas time. We get donations as small as a few

tins of spaghetti up to pallets of stock from big business. We love and appreciate every little bit!

We then have a big packing day where we pack and deliver boxes filled with goodies to the families in need. We work with existing charities and ask them who needs help. They supply a list of families.

It brings me such joy to deliver the hampers and see the looks on the people's faces!

One that I will always remember was a lady in her mid 30's, (not much older than me!) who had five kids under 7. Her husband had just died suddenly with no insurance and had left her with five children and a massive amount of debt. She had just moved back in with her parents because she could not afford the rent without her husband's wages.

When we deliver the hampers all we say is, "Someone that loves you very much would like you to have a wonderful Christmas, and hopes that you will be able to look after yourself so that you can help someone else out one day." When they realize that the boxes are filled with food and toys for the kids, some of them are so overwhelmed that they start crying before they even open the box. This is a really beautiful way to start the Christmas season.

The packing day is usually 1-3 weeks before Christmas and it gives me that warm fuzzy feeling for weeks, knowing that I have made a difference in the lives of about 3,000 people at Christmas.

Visit www.magicmoments.org.au if you would like to find out more or would be able to help ☺

Last year I also joined a travel club that has a really cool foundation that does voluntours, like building bottle schools in Guatemala, renovating orphanages in Thailand, building basketball courts and making over boys and girls clubs in the USA. What better way to go on holidays and be able to help people and communities that need a hand up not a hand out. We are even doing them here in Australia too helping local children.

Holidays and charity two of my greatest pleasures rolled into one...

* List 5 things I am grateful for every day.

I have been doing this mentally for years now. Every morning when I wake up and every night before I go to sleep, I think of at least 5 things I'm grateful for. You can also use a Gratitude Journal App on your phone or Ipad or invest in a journal and use it as a diary of the amazing things that happen in my life. I like to get one's that have a beautiful cover or you can decorate it your self. It is great as a reference for when you are having a down day you can look back and look at all the things that you are grateful for and realize how blessed your life really is you can get out of your pity party a lot quicker and get back to enjoying the blessed life you have. You can also use a gratitude jar with post-it notes – and pull them out on NEW YEARS EVE and read about your awesome year.

* The past does not equal the future unless we let it.

So many people live in the past. This is crazy!
You can't change the past so move on. Yes, bad things happen to good people. But you can't keep living that over and over again.

Just because one person breaks your heart does not mean that every partner will do the same. Don't blame or let people in your past affect the relationships in the present and the future. If I lived my life knowing that in every relationship the guy will leave me, I would never take a chance on a new one. Everyone is different.
Don't judge the people in your present by the people in your past. You need to live and learn from your past and not relive it! If you continue to live in the past, your future will be the same. So it is now time to change your future.

Every day is a new day! You need to live your life that way! Stop beating yourself up over the actions and decisions of your past!
Unless you have a time machine you can't change it, so deal with it and move on.
I have been dumped or rejected by guys more times than anyone I know, and if I hear one more time
" It's Not You, It's Me," or, " I'm Not Ready For A Relationship," I think I will vomit ...LOL..
But as many times as I hear that (and its been a lot), it does not stop me from getting back in the game and finding the next "Mr. Right Now."

People come into our life for a reason, a season or a lifetime. Sometimes, even if we want that person to be there for a lifetime, but the universe only sent them to us for a season or a reason. When a relationship ends, you have two choices:

1. You can sit in a corner and cry, "Why me," "Poor me," or "Why do I always get my heart broken," "why doesn't he love me? Why am I not good enough" And be miserable for days, weeks, or months.
2. Or you can do what I do and say, "Thank you." Yes, you heard me correctly. I say, "THANK YOU!" (Not usually to them – but just to the universe). I thank the universe for bringing them into my life so I could share those magical moments with them, even if it was not for very long. Some of my most magical relationships have only lasted a few weeks. It is not about the quantity of time you spend with someone, it is about the quality of time you spend with them.
3. Next! By releasing them from your life and your heart you are making room for the next person to enter,
   While you are still emotionally still attached to your ex you cannot make room for someone new.

I thank the universe for bringing them into my life to teach me whatever lesson I needed to learn, for sharing whatever experience I needed to have, and for the passion and great sex that I wanted to have.
Then I thank the universe for ending the relationship. This has now made room for someone even more wonderful to come into my life!

Let me repeat that so that it sinks in: I thank the universe for the time we shared and ending the relationship peacefully so that I now have space available to let in a new relationship that will fill my heart with even more love and passion and amazing magical moments.

Yes I still get upset when a relationship ends, but I don't hang on to that pain for long. I release it and thank the universe for bringing them into my life in the first place so that I could share what we had, even if it I didn't think it was long enough. The universe had other plans for me, so we headed in a different direction. If you have struggled over relationships please read over this section a few times till it sinks in.. Put your hand on your heart (GO ON DO IT)
With you hand on your heart take a few deep breaths and think about someone that has broken your heart, now. Thank the universe for allowing you to meet them to experience the good times you had and to learn what ever lessons you needed to learn (sometimes you will never consciously know what they are, but they universe does, xx trust it) And now thank the universe for releasing them from your life and heart, so that you can fill it with love and joy from someone new.

You are AMAZING and deserve to be worshipped by the love of your life, don't ever settle for a mediocre life or relationship, Life is too short to not expect the best from yourself and others.

Now don't get me wrong I'm not saying that you need to reject people from your life but what I am saying is have a look at who is in your life, your physical relationships, your friendship relationships, your family relationships & your working relationships?

- Do these people make you want to be a better person when you are around them?
- Do they encourage you to achieve things?
- Do they congratulate you when you succeed?

    Or

- Are they always belittling you, making you feel less worthy than you are?
- Do they tell you your hopes and dreams are silly and stupid? Are they a dream stealer?
- Are you always worried about what they are going to think about what you do, think or say? Even though every time they make you feel bad?

Its time to step up and make a choice now! Are you going to sit in the back seat of the car called your life and let other people decide where you are going and how fast or how slow you are going If you are going to get there at all?

Or is it time that you get in the driver's seat OF YOUR AMAZING LIFE, grab the wheel and put your foot down before you run out of petrol. Life is so short and so precious, trust me I've seen it being in hospital room with people connected to life support machines, in the blink of an eye, you can be living your life and the next thing you are a vegetable from a car accident, a king hit or an aneurism. Tell your loved ones you love them, spend time with people that inspire you to live a better life, and always

Live with Passion, Purpose, Love & Gratitude

Nikki Galagher
AKA NikkiBlu

About the author

I have had many jobs and careers in my lifetime spanning across many industries such as Hospitality, Personal Development Education, Beauty, fashion, travel and party plan to name a few... I have loved every job i have ever had as i believe you should love what you do or there is no point doing it. You spend 1/3 of your life at work so you should love what you do.

I love Fashion and everything about it and currently work as an instore Stylist for Chic Chic - one of Australia's most popular Plus Size fashion stores, i love making woman feel beautiful about their bodies and looking fabulous in the clothes they wear.

I am a Sexpert – an Expert in Sex, Orgasms & Pleasure. I'm a business owner and consultant with Horny Little Devils Australia's #1 Voted Adult Toy & Lingerie Party plan company.
If you like it a little Bit Naughty www.nikkiblu.com

I have always loved to travel and love getting bargains, so when the opportunity to become an independent business representative with the world's leading wholesale travel company was offered to me, i jumped at the chance it was a no brainer.. Who doesn't love cheap travel and the opportunity to make money while you are doing it.
If you love to travel check out www.nikkiblutravel.com

While i love Sex, fashion & travel, I have many passions including but not limited to writing, personal development, internet business & marketing, Learning new skills, being creative, cooking & entertaining, shopping for a bargain and of course i love my friends and family.

I consider myself a...

- Wonderful Friend
- Sensational Lover
- Awesome Daughter, sister,
- Sexpert,
- Plus size -Stylist
- 6X Brain Surgery Survivor
- Published Author & Mentor
- World Traveler
- Amazing home cook
- 10+ Year Seminar Junkie
- And all round AMAZING chic
- just to name a few .....

So everyday live with
Love & Gratitude and
Passion & Purpose

Being in 'Love and Gratitude' Over a Death of a Loved One

Just a few short years ago if I had read this heading I would have thought that the author had gone 'bonkers' or had inherited a fortune; hence the love and gratitude. Due to my naivety or lack of awareness I would have thought; how could anyone have love and/or gratitude in regards to a death of a loved one?

Though now, nearly four years after an unexpected tragedy, I now have a newfound awareness and understand that there is Love and Gratitude to be found in every event that occurs in our lives, even a perceived negative event, as and when we choose to look for it.

Many years ago, when I first read Napoleon Hill's legendary book 'Think and Grow Rich" I can clearly remember reading, and resonating with this quote "Every adversity, every failure, every heartache carries with it the seed of an equal or greater benefit." I even remember where I was when I read this as I contemplated how true it is. And then I continued on my merry way categorizing people and events as *good or bad*, *fun or sad*, and *my fault or their fault*, never looking deeper into the reason why things were happening to me.

Though now, I spend each day, each moment to be more accurate, asking myself "Why did I create this (event, situation), what am I meant to learn, where I am meant to heal, what is my lesson from this?" whenever a perceived negative event or comment comes into my space.

If there was one special gift I would give anyone, it would be for them to understand this concept when they are in their late teens / early twenties. As it's the most liberating and fulfilling way to live each day.

Waking up, Never to Be the Same Again.

On the 10th July 2011, my husband, Andrew, and I, we were in no hurry to jump out of bed as we had planned a lazy Sunday morning. Around 8.30 a.m., we decided maybe we should get up and have some breakfast.

Whilst I started to heat up some leftovers from the night before, Andrew decided to take the rubbish out to the bins, so he went downstairs and opened the back door.

He shouted out to me: "Bloody hell, Daniel (our 27 year old son) is passed out at the back door." A big alarm bell went off in my head, as this was really unusual. Yes, at times Dan did drink too much, though he always made it home and into his own bed.

At the time, Dan and his girlfriend, Georgie, were living with us and they had just started looking around to find their own place to rent. They had both gone out separately the night before, Georgie to a work function and Dan with some friends.

I ran down the stairs without even touching them and kneeled by his side. Dan was lying on his left side in a foetal position. I started to shake him, "Dan, Dan wake up." He had blood on his face and saliva coming out of his mouth, so I thought he had been beaten up and was just unconscious.

Alas, this was not the case; he had actually passed away several hours before.

This was the start of the new phase of my life. As tragic as Dan's passing was, I am a better person because of it and I love the person I have become.

Now, please, don't misunderstand me. I wish Dan was still here, making me laugh, annoying me, growing and fulfilling his life, and sharing his ideas and plans for the future. Though, as that is not possible, I have chosen to see all the good he is doing from the other side.

Finding Your Unique Healing Process

When your child passes away, the pain and devastation of your loss can feel overwhelming.

Dan was my youngest child, my baby – by one minute. Dan has a twin brother, Josh, and an older brother, Ben.

Every individual will process grief in their own unique way. My husband, Andrew (Dan's father), and I coped with our son's passing completely differently.

There is no "right" or "wrong" way to grieve. I am sharing my story as bereaved parents may find it helpful to have some guidance and support along the way.

Some of the immediate emotions in grief are shock, numbness, denial, confusion and disbelief—all of which can act as a cushion against the full impact of your loss.

As time passes, some of these early emotions may begin to wear off as others emerge including guilt, anger, loneliness, despair, sadness and regret. Because of the intensity of all of the emotions you are feeling, you may not be able to fully comprehend all that you are experiencing. These feelings and emotions are all a normal and natural response to the passing of someone you love.

Some will express their pain easily and openly, while others will keep their feelings locked inside.

For me, a major coping mechanism was that I have always believed that we all come to Earth to fulfill a purpose and to serve our fellow humans. We may be here for a little while or for a century. The length of time we are here does not equate to the amount of difference we can make.

Dan was here for 27 years and he made a difference. He was lucky enough to have travelled and saw many parts of the world. I was amazed at how many lives he had touched all around the globe. His sudden passing sent many a hardened man to find some "alone time" for a few hours.

As much as I loved being his mother and having him here, I also know that personally he has helped me more toward "fulfilling my purpose" since his passing than he did whilst he was in this realm.

My Awakening - Being True to Me

At the time of Dan's passing, I was a Chief Financial Officer (CFO) of a publicly listed company. I loved my life, though in hindsight I was actually, working too much, drinking too much and definitely eating too much. I was very much in a *"ground hog day daze"* and I did not even realise it.

I was perceived as being very successful; I had the job, the salary, the contacts, the house, the car, the family and the overseas holidays. Though in reality I was not empowered in all seven areas of my life i.e. mentally, professionally, financially, socially, family, physically and spiritually.

As I did know how to be a grieving mother, I immediately went back to work after Dan's funeral. I engrossed myself into my job, working even longer hours.

Of course, the universe was not happy with me ignoring, the *first knock on the door* for me to start empowering all areas of my life, so about 15 months later I was made redundant (laid off) from my CFO role.

Even though this was my choice, for a couple of days, I went into the blame-game and how dare they do this to me. Then as I started to come out of the *"ground hog day daze"*, I started to realise that this may be the best thing that ever happened to me.

That is right; I had time to take a breath, a long deep belly breath. You know the one, when you slowly breathe in you feel like you are getting a new sense of *hope & vitality* and as you breathe out you feel you are releasing all the *stale energy* that has been keeping you *stuck, unfulfilled & un-energised*.

Within weeks of me taking the first of many of those breaths, I found myself at a BraveHeart Women Global Community, four day event in LA called RiseLA2012.

BraveHeart Women is a community where we Collaborate - Joyously, Prosperously, Harmoniously, so you can BE, CREATE and COLLABORATE.

BraveHeart Women global community offers the tools, courses, connection and collaborative energy essential for you to truly express your authentic self.

For four days I nodded in agreement as Ellie Drake (founder) shared many gems, like:

- Key to joy, prosperity and fulfillment; Live your life on Purpose – Personally, Professionally and Globally;
- Move from survival to thriving
- Adrenalin does not work in a woman's body
- Say NO, to misaligned projects and people; gain extra time and energy
- Learn to receive, starting with a compliment, prosperity will follow

I jumped at the opportunity to be trained so I could become a BraveHeart Woman Resonator and start building community in Australia.

I honestly started to feel (and now 'know') that Dan had me by the shoulders, guiding me this way and that, saying *"Ok Mum, you never listened to me when I was alive, now is the time for you to empower all areas of your life, live on purpose and start to become the woman you came here to be, namely **serve people and make a difference.**"*

Very quickly I began to realise how much easier my life would have been if I had these tools whilst I was a CFO. I would have had more joy, passion, energy, time, been more productive and every relationship would have been better. I also started to realise how much more conducive the workplace would have been, as everyone would have followed my lead. Yes I did a disservice to my company by not realising that the health of the bottom line is directly correlated to the health of the employees.

Sharing My Many Lessons

Over the past 30 months I have meet many amazing people who have assisted me to grow and learn many lessons. I guess one of the most profound philosophy is that *"when the student is ready the teacher will appear,"* and humbly I feel that may be why you are reading this chapter now.

Before I expand upon some of my challenges, achievements and lessons I have learned, I feel it's very apt for us to review the Laws of the Universe.

The Laws of the Universe

We are all spiritual beings having an earthly experience. So, it is always good as we journey through life, and especially while on the road to becoming our own best friends, to be consciously aware of the Laws of the Universe.

It is also great to realise that everyone faces struggles and challenges, especially when we decide to step up and become the person we came here to be. These challenges are just the universe testing us to see if we are serious, we're not just trying to fake it till we make it. The universe wants to make sure we have taken the leap, The Leap of Faith, so to speak.

There are 12 universal laws. I have seen them written in numerous publications, though one of my favourites is from Milanovich and McCunes book The Light Shall Set You Free (1998), so here is an excerpt:

1. **The Law of Divine Oneness**: The first out of the 12 universal Laws helps us to understand that we live in a world where everything is connected to everything else. Everything we do, say, think and believe affects others and the universe around us.

2. **The Law of Vibration:** This Law states that everything in the universe moves, vibrates, and travels in circular patterns. The same principles of vibration in the physical world apply to our thoughts, feelings, desires, and wills in the etheric world. Each sound, thing, and even thought has its own vibrational frequency, unique unto itself.

3. **The Law of Action:** The Law of Action must be applied in order for us to manifest things on earth. Therefore, we must engage in actions that support our thoughts, dreams, emotions and words.

4. **The Law of Correspondence**: This Law states that the principles or laws of physics that explain the physical world – energy, light, vibration, and motion – have their corresponding principles in the etheric or universe. "As above, so below."

5. **The Law of Cause and Effect**: This Law states that nothing happens by chance or outside the Universal Laws. Every action has a reaction or consequence and we "reap what we have sown."

6. **The Law of Compensation**: This Law is the Law of Cause and Effect applied to blessings and abundance that are provided for us. The visible effects of our deeds are given to us in gifts, money, inheritances, friendships, and blessings.

7. **The Law of Attraction**: This Law demonstrates how we create the things, events, and people that come into our lives. Our thoughts, feelings, words, and actions produce energies which, in turn, attract like energies. Negative energies attract negative energies and positive energies attract positive energies.

8. **The Law of Perpetual Transmutation of Energy**: This 8th law out of the 12 Universal Laws is a powerful one. It states that all persons have within them the power to change the conditions in their lives. Higher vibrations consume and transform lower ones; thus, each of us can change the energies in our lives by understanding the Universal Laws and applying the principles in such a way as to effect change.

9. **The Law of Relativity:** This Law states that each person will receive a series of problems (Tests of Initiation) for the purpose of strengthening the Light within. We must consider each of these tests to be a challenge and remain connected to our hearts when proceeding to solve the problems. This law also teaches us to compare our problems to others' problems and put everything into its proper perspective. No matter how bad we perceive our situation to be, there is always someone who is in a worse position. It is all relative.

10. **The Law of Polarity**: This Law states that everything is on a continuum and has an opposite. We can suppress and transform undesirable thoughts by concentrating on the opposite pole. It is the law of mental vibrations.

11. **The Law of Rhythm:** This Law states that everything vibrates and moves to certain rhythms. These rhythms establish seasons, cycles, stages of development, and patterns. Each cycle reflects the regularity of God's universe. Masters know how to rise above negative parts of a cycle by never getting too excited or allowing negative things to penetrate their consciousness.

12. **The Law of Gender:** This last out of the 12 Universal Laws states that everything has its masculine (yang) and feminine (yin) principles, and that these are the basis for all creation. The spiritual Initiate must balance the masculine and feminine energies within herself or himself to become a Master and a true co-creator with God.

I love reading these laws. I love understanding these laws. I love living according to the laws.

The key to living a fulfilled, happy, joyous, prosperous and empowered life is to consciously have these laws as a key daily focus, especially when you feel "life is out to get you and you can't do anything right."

I now have a knowing that I am here to serve and the more I give the more I will receive what I desire. I have a givers: gain philosophy.

With this in mind, I'm sure you'll receive many gems as you read my perceived challenges, perceived achievements and the many, many lessons I've learnt along my path.

My Perceived Challenges

- **Embracing my feminine side:** Previously I never realised what a disservice I was doing to myself, family and company that employed me by not honouring and staying true to my feminine innate qualities. Sure you require your masculine (Law 12) in order to get a head and to create though you should only be going in and out, not living that way. Now I look after myself in many ways, all of my relationships have improved and I love and value being a woman. My daily tools have assisted me greatly in this area.

- **Understanding the Laws of the Universe and Divine time:** It took a while for me to fully embrace living each day this way. Changing the focus from *outer to within* to *from within to outer* is so liberating. No longer any requirement for the blame-game!!! Divine time is to realise that you will receive what you want though it will be when the time is right. This may be later than you expected so the key is live with trust and faith with no attachment, then more than likely what you receive is far beyond your original expectations.

- **Moving from Ego to Essence:** Ego is such a lack-mindset focus. It is *my way or no way*. Once you start to honour yourself and live in your Essence, you start to realise that there are multiple ways to do everything and collaboration is the key. No one has traveled this path before, so why are we so sure that our way is the right way? By Essence I mean "The essence of life" It's to be in constant growth. Every day, I remind myself to keep moving, to be open to change, to all possibilities, to keep enquiring and try to be better than yesterday me."

- **Understanding that you will always receive more No's than Yes's:** This takes a while to understand and to embrace. When you are starting a new business it can be very debilitating when you continue to get "No's" though once you start to change the focus to *"Ok, I'm one step closer to a Yes"*, that assists you to keep moving forward and take daily action steps.

*

My Perceived Achievements

- **Spending the first 45 mins of each day on me:** This is the key to having more time, energy and your success. You'll literally *tap dance* to and from work every day.
- **Daily being so joyous, happy and fulfilled:** Life is a choice. The more you focus on this, the more you will live this way.
- **Recognising that all my relationships have positively grown:** I consciously make sure that I am empowering each of the seven areas of my life. What you focus on grows.
- **Embracing speaking – Having a passionate message – is Key!!:** I always had a voice though not the message. Now that I know my purpose is to *Inspire Women to Empowerment in all areas of their lives,* I've become a passionate and inspirational speaker.
- **Writing and self publishing two books (third will be publish mid 2015):** Busting through this limiting belief has been amazing. I receive so much joy and fulfillment through my writing and know that there are many more books to come.
- **Connecting with many inspirational, like- minded people:** I have so many new found friends networks and connections in my life. It is hard to look back and realise how insular I was before.

*

Lessons I've have learnt
- Everything I require is inside me
- We are all UNIQUE. Stop comparing
- What you think about me is none of my business
- Embrace the negative and positive. Celebrate both equally. This is growth.
- By helping others, you get what you want.
- Forgive yourself
- There is no competition for your true life purpose
- Be open to all possibilities
- If it's not working; change it

The Essence of My Life:
Before I close, I would like to share and reiterate that they key to life is to be of service. Once we have a givers/gain focus we can live our life in our Essence. It's important to realise that your Essence will be different to mine

and anyone else's as it stems from lifelong, personal experiences and lessons learned.

For me my Essence is; To live my life in Love & Gratitude; To continually create new experiences; To Be my unique self; To Live in the moment; To Be positive; To have fun; To Invest in ME, quality time, quality relationships; To Evolve-Learn-Grow

In summary, the essence of life is constant growth. Every day, I remind myself to keep moving, to be open to change, to all possibilities, to keep inquiring and to try to better than yesterday me."

Does that make sense?

In fact, some people go through an entire lifetime, missing the gist of it— lost in their daily routine, disoriented in their demanding life and focusing on materialism.

One of Wayne Dyer (American inspirational speaker) quote is *"Don't die with your music still in you."*

I would probably rephrase that to *"Die after you have lived your life in Essence."*

Thank you for reading my story, I trust you enjoyed it as much I did sharing it.

With Love and Gratitude

Karen Chaston

About the Author

Karen Chaston: *"Inspiring Women to Empower all Areas of their Lives"*

Surprisingly, it took her son's death for her to become more aware, grateful, healthier, energised and live in her Essence.

With a wealth of knowledge and experience amassed over the course of an illustrious 20-year career in leadership and business, Karen was perceived to be very successful, actually she was living a *ground hog day existence*, running on empty, not fulfilled, and not understanding that adrenalin in a woman's body causes burnout, exhaustion, and disconnectedness.

Karen now inspires women to become their own best friend, to live in their Essence and be empowered in all areas of their lives. When women believe in themselves and have high self-esteem it is amazing what they can accomplish.

Karen utilises many forums; speaking, writing, radio host, one-to-one mentoring, and group coaching and training programs to deliver "*The new model of the feminine*" programs. These programs provide a deeper connection and a profound understanding of the multi-faceted components that make up a woman and her life.

Karen's ideal clients are leaders and managers in the world's most progressive businesses that recognise that the health and prosperity of their business is directly correlated to the health of their employees, namely their female employees.

The programs help guide your colleagues away from burnout, exhaustion and competition towards more energised, engaged, motivated, collaborative and productive employees who have a CEO oriented focus. This ultimately leads to a more conducive work environment, more profits for the company, increased corporate image with an increased attraction and retention of staff.

Karen is passionate about creating more "conscious entrepreneurs"; who allow heart and soul, as well as knowledge and expertise, to guide their businesses.

Karen Chaston
Sydney Australia
www.karenchaston.com.au

Beating Bipolar Disorder

In June 2008 I was diagnosed with Bipolar Disorder type 1 and the world, as I knew it changed forever.

Looking back I had all the classic signs which started to become more prevalent in my early to mid twenties – highly emotional, dysfunctional relationships, excessive spending, promiscuous, drug and alcohol abuse etc. but I did the best I could to manage.

Growing up I think I always knew I was different, just not sure in what way. I was an only child who had an incredibly close relationship with my mother and grandparents and always felt loved. I treasured my life. I had minor episodes during my teens, without realising what they were. It was only in hindsight, when discussing it with my mum, did we realise that these episodes were probably the start of my Bipolar.

I was never exposed to violence, drug or alcohol addiction or any form of abuse and only discovered later that there was a history of mental illness on my father's side of the family.

I was social, ambitious and had accomplished a lot. I was lucky enough to be awarded a scholarship to the Australian Defence Force Academy in 1996. I was also involved in the making of a TV Pilot and was the touring PR Manager for basketball legend Dennis Rodman when he came to Australia in early 2008. My future looked bright, or so it seemed.

Prior to my diagnosis, I had a number of roles as a Sales & Marketing Manager in property development companies. I was well paid, had a great social life and thought my existence was relatively normal... well for me anyway.

During all of this, I continued to have "episodes" but didn't think anything of them at the time. I just thought I was normal. My mother described it as my "going off the rails" but we never even gave it a thought that I had a mental illness.
I was always super sensitive and highly emotional, which would lead to exaggerated responses to situations. What was normal to me wasn't for most people. This caused a great deal of havoc with relationships and my day to day life.

I was initially diagnosed with depression and was put on anti-depressants, which made me feel worse. I had been seeing a psychologist irregularly to help with managing my day-to-day life. It all came to a head late one night. I was sitting in bed crying, feeling helpless and hopeless, and not understanding the thoughts and confusion in my head. I didn't want to die, but I wanted those feelings of distress to stop. I went to the kitchen with the intent to self-harm and as I went to draw the knife along my wrist, my cat jumped up on the kitchen bench and just sat there and looked at me purring. I'll never forget that, and in that moment, it gave me strength to reach out.

That next day I called my mum and we arranged for a more thorough assessment of my psyche and was initially diagnosed with Bipolar Disorder Type 2. I was told however that I wouldn't require therapy but was placed on a mood stabiliser

Initially I was told that I would require medication for two years then should be ok after that. What a joke that was! Although I was on medication (most of the time) I still went through episodes which saw me slide downhill into some pretty dark places, but did manage to climb my way out with the help of regular medication, support from family and counselling.

Over the next couple of years, I took my medication and continued to see a psychologist and developed my creative side, which gave me some peace and stability.

In 2010 I moved from Brisbane to Gold Coast to pursue my hobby in Fashion Styling as I had started to explore my love of fashion and had developed a bit of a profile. I was still unstable and experienced the traditional highs and lows associated with Bipolar.

It wasn't until my move to the Gold Coast that I was referred to a GP that specialised in mental health. He was the turning point in getting real answers to my condition. It was then that I was assessed by a Psychiatrist with a new diagnosis of Bipolar Disorder Type 1. The main difference between Type 1 and Type 2 is the prevalence of more manic episodes as opposed to depressive episodes, with Type 1 being more severe. The prognosis wasn't good. I was advised I would have to spend the rest of my life on medication and would require regular visits with psychiatrists and psychologists, and the chances of me being able to be employed full time again was slim to none. I had to completely change my lifestyle. I was devastated, but determined to listen to the specialists and do whatever was needed to be well.

I was heavily in debt as a result of reckless and impulsive spending during my manic states which was pre-diagnosis and during my initial treatment, so was still financially responsible for keeping on top of my bills. This added severely to the stress of my everyday life. Because I lived alone and had no family in town, it had been easy to hide my addictions and destructive behaviour. It took me over five years to be financially stable and to learn how to manage my money and control my impulsiveness.

By 2013, still on a small amount of medication with a relatively low dosage and seeing a psychiatrist only (monthly), I was doing some contract work for a magazine as a Fashion and Lifestyle Stylist and had built myself quite a portfolio, all the while blogging about fashion and life. Things were good.

In Jan-June 2013, I was advised to increase my medication and was introduced to new medication (anti–psychotic, sleeping and anti-anxiety) to deal with a new romance, as I had been single for seven years – it was a massive adjustment for me, and I had been suffering insomnia and severe paranoia. Over the next 12 months my behaviour changed dramatically and during that time, I was taking up to 17 pills a day as prescribed. My episodes started to become more regular and more dangerous and I developed what's known as "rapid cycling", I became aggressive and even psychotic which was completely out of character. My paranoia started to affect my work with the Magazine as well as my relationship with my boyfriend, and by December that year I had to end my contract with the Magazine to focus on my health, which was upsetting as the creative work, was a huge part of my therapy.

For the first time in my life I actually believed I was going crazy. It was terrifying. I experienced feelings of hopelessness that left me feeling numb or confused and angry. I couldn't see the light at the end of the tunnel.

I voiced my concerns a number of times and was advised to increase my medication again and have more regular visits with the specialists. I had lost sight of who I was and became completely consumed by my illness. It was all I thought about, and the main topic of conversation in my life, especially with those close to me.

I questioned everything about myself. Every thought and every action. Is this the real me or is this the Bipolar? What would I be like if I didn't have this mental illness? What would my life be like? Would I still be funny or creative? I felt like I had lost so many years.

I soon learnt that the good, the bad and the ugly of Bipolar was part of me and it didn't have to control me.

It has taken a great deal of therapy and insight to understand the difference and to recognise triggers.

But I was a fighter, I was determined to be well and wanted to do whatever was needed.

I had decided to open up about my Bipolar as I had experienced a great deal of negative stigma associated with having a mental illness and had decided that I wanted to work towards educating and creating awareness.

People in my life struggled to deal with my erratic behaviour that often made me come across as needy. It's hard to explain your feelings and moods to someone when you can't understand them yourself. As a result I have lost a lot of friends over the years and was often referred to as high maintenance or difficult. A great deal of the time, people thought they could "save me" when all I needed was a great support network standing by me while I saved myself.

For the first few years on the Gold Coast I was seeing an amazing psychologist that I really connected with. She helped me to understand the behaviours associated with Bipolar and taught me how to deal with stressful situations. She also taught me how to accept the illness and myself, as I experienced feelings of grief and denial at times.

Unfortunately, she went on maternity leave, which left me to find a new therapist. I was referred to a male psychologist who I was unable to build a relationship with and stopped seeking help. This had a huge impact on me and I mourned for that connection and talk therapy.

2014 things just went from bad to worse and my life was a living hell, dealing with almost weekly episodes that would have me unable to function day to day. I lost my outgoing nature, sense of humour, motivation and ambition. I was so unhappy and could see no future at all for myself. Suicidal thoughts were regular. It was common for me to not sleep for as many as four days and became delusional, imagining conversations and events that never happened. Most days just getting out of bed took every ounce of strength I had. My greatest accomplishments at times was just having a shower or having a day when I didn't cry.

Strangely the tears weren't from feelings of depression, but confusion. Confusion that my behaviour and feelings weren't my own, and I had no control over my day-to-day actions.

When I would rage, I would totally lose control, becoming a passenger to my mind and body. Afterwards feeling shame and guilt once I found out the things I had said or done, and it was always to the ones I loved the most.

I would become argumentative and aggressive, incredibly cruel and hurtful then not have any memory of the events. Those episodes would take me days to recover because of the intensity. It was a vicious cycle.

Not only did I have to deal with the emotional symptoms, but the daily physiological side effects from the medication. This included uncontrollable bowel movements, excessive thirst and urination, tingling in my extremities and regular eye twitching.

I had another suicide attempt in October 2014, thankfully intercepted by my boyfriend, which was a terrifying experience, as again my legitimate feelings and wants were not ones of death but just wanting to stop the torture going on inside my head. I still can't remember that night very clearly. It's like a blackout.

By then I knew there was something seriously wrong as my behaviour did not match my inner feelings and I started to question my medication.

I made the decision to go off one of them and things started to get better. I reached out to my specialists and was nearly shipped off to the mental health unit, which I knew was the worst possible thing for me. Fortunately my GP was supportive of my decision.

Then in November 2014, I had started to develop severe physical symptoms such as swelling of the feet and face, impaired vision, impaired speech, poor balance, tingling in my limbs, increased paranoia, shortness of breath and was behaving extremely erratically. I was also struggling to walk. The physical symptoms worsened and after a visit to the doctor for a blood test to assess my blood lithium levels, I was rushed to hospital by ambulance on 1 December 2014.

It was discovered that I had lithium toxicity and it was at such a high level it was extremely dangerous and at worst, could have been fatal. The lithium (mood stabiliser) was poisoning my blood and had been causing not only the physical symptoms, but had been the root of my behavioural changes and also the psychotic break that led to the suicide attempt. My kidneys were so damaged that dialysis was being considered as an option and my thyroid was underactive (which had explained the 30kg I had put on over the years). I had also experienced neurological damage and was unable to walk or see very well for a number of weeks after being discharged.

During my seven-day stay in hospital, I was flushed of all the chemicals from the medication in my body. I received unbelievably good treatment from the physicians and carers whilst there, who discussed my ongoing care and management of my illness.

I've been medication free since the day of admission and I've never felt better. I've been focusing on developing my own coping strategies such as healthy eating, stress management, exercise and have also incorporated super foods into my diet. I've had no episodes of any kind and feel fantastic. It's like a whole new world. The medication that was supposed to be "helping" me was actually making me crazy and could have killed me.

I still see my GP regularly, who has been extremely supportive through the last few years. I have regular blood tests to check on my levels, ensuring that everything is normal.

I am now intent on raising awareness on mental health issues and telling my story through my blog and every way possible in the hopes of helping others.

I'm excited that I've also been selected as a speaker for SANE Australia www.sane.org , the national charity that raises awareness on mental health issues and campaigns to stop the stigma.

I have regained my love for writing and fashion and this has helped me immensely with my recovery, as I believe creative therapy is a fantastic form of stress relief. All About Missy www.missyrobinson.com.au has been a great outlet for sharing my experience as well as being that creative passage. I've also recently launched the only Australian online boutique through a global social fashion revolution called Zindigo; which offers billions of social media users around the globe the opportunity to partner with luxury brands and designers, and open their own free, fully merchandised social boutique.

As a result of my journey I have learnt that there are so many ways to deal with managing your mental health whether you chose the pharmaceutical route, natural therapy or an integrated approach.

I want to inspire and give hope to those out there who may be experiencing the same thing. I am more than my Bipolar, and I want to be able to educate those about the illness as well as stop the stigma attached to it.

Missy Robinson

About the author

Stylist, writer, blogger and speaker – Missy Robinson is an enlightened soul, as evidenced by her chic and unique sense of style, and her passion for sharing insights that are beyond skin deep.

All About Missy is dedicated to sharing all things in 'fashion' and 'lifestyle' that are fabulous and cool, but Missy has also opened up this space to reflect more about her day to day life and overcoming adversity living with Bipolar Disorder.

Missy is proud to be an advocate for raising awareness about mental health, and has been selected as a speaker for SANE Australia, the national mental health charity.

She has worked professionally with numerous high profile lifestyle and beauty brands, events, popular women's consumer magazines, celebrities, and many fashion designers and labels. Her portfolio is expanding however with the opening of her online fashion boutique Zindigo.

An internationally published fashion stylist and featured writer of food and travel, Missy is open to new opportunities to share her love of creativity and the benefits it can have to a positive and healthy mind, body and spirit.

How to overcome challenges

Only now do I realise just how bad things really are... I'm sitting wide awake in a bed in Australia 15000 km away from my secure home in Sweden. I'm in country where I know absolutely no one. No friends, no family, no one to call on for comfort and support. I reluctantly reach for my laptop to look at my finances. I have all of $70 in my bank account, my email is full of final notices for my delayed rent payments. I have no ticket back to Sweden and without any social security or help from the government and no one who would even care if I had a roof over my head or not, I begin to become very anxious. My heart sinks.

For the last few months all of my money has been invested in personal development seminars around the world. So even though I sit here in a panic over how broke I am, my mind is so full of riches. I have gained so much valuable information about how to become a successful person, when I think of it I realise how backwards it may sound. But my mentors always told me how important these seminars are and that you should never stop learning or growing, as this is vital in making you a successful person. I never did doubt that things I have learned from these insightful seminars could transform my life, but I did began to wonder, when would it be my turn?

I really need to fix this situation now! I desperately start to look for a loan from a safe bank. Since I'm a Swedish citizen living in Australia as an exchange student I encountered many complications. Firstly, I could only borrow money from Swedish banks which limited my options. I also was unable to show any evidence of a secure income. Still, I tried and tried and tried. Each time I would apply for a new loan at a different bank, it was saved in a database which all banks could access. It didn't take long for the banks to discover just how desperate I was. Everyone denied me.

This left me with one final option that I could see... Ask to borrow money from my family. It took a lot for me to be able do this as I hate asking people for money, but I saw no other option. So I swallowed my pride and contacted my mother and father. They already knew that I had received a $10 000 loan from the government before I left Sweden to begin my exchange studies in Australia, so of course they were wondering where it had all gone. I had nothing to physically show them, just my travels and seminars. They both refused me. I want to underline though that months later I did appreciate their decision. However, at the time this made me feel so alone. At this point I truly had nothing, not even security from my family. I had no one to turn to for help anymore.

Fear begins to succumb me as my anxiousness becomes so uncontrollable that I begin shaking. My brain goes into panic mode. This is without a doubt, one of the worst moments of my life. I have just been told that I am completely on my own, helpless. A horrible thought flashed by my eyes, is this the end for me?

Now I want to take you back to where my life started to divide itself from the people around me.
I have always created my own path in life and have rarely listened to anybody else or cared what they thought. I believe this skill has both helped and hindered me.

At the age of sixteen I moved out from my parents home to a new city a couple of hours away from the little village I grew up in. I was seen as a very talented handball player and fought my way into one of the best sports schools in Sweden. I had to grow up almost instantly when I moved out on my own. I went from having a lifestyle where everything was served to me on a silver platter to having to do everything for myself. This was quite a big change for me.

I started to see how much I stood out from my surroundings. Since I had moved and had to grow up so much faster than all my classmates, there was a big gap between us. I began to find them very immature, so for most of the time I was on my own as I did not want to become like them. This ended up being a very wise decision for me, for my teachers started to notice and appreciate me as being a very good student.

After having done so much personal development I can now understand why this happened. The teachers saw me as a student that stood out from the rest and performed well in class. This became my new identity, and when everyone starts to see/treat you in a certain way you will start to do things that match that identity. My grades became really good thanks to that. I could also see the same things happening in my sports life. To grow up in a locker room normally forms you a lot as a teenager, but I never let myself fall into that stereotype. I always stood up for what I thought and believed in even though this led to some of my teammates bullying me.

Things got worse when our new trainer was introduced to the team as he would always pick on all the younger players, myself included. Ultimately, this is one of the reasons which led me to discontinue my very promising handball career. However, after reading my first personal development book "How to think and grow rich" written by Napoleon Hill, the main reason has become clear as to why I did not pursue this career. I was lacking in one of the most crucial ingredients in Hill's success recipe which was having a burning desire for what you do. He would always say how "the man who thinks he can and the man who thinks he can't are both right". I found this to be a 100% true.

Don't get me wrong, I loved handball and I had all the right conditions to succeed with free access to the gym twice a day, nutritious food and a great trainer (apart from the last one), yet I still chose to quit due to this small challenge which stood in my way. If I truly had a burning desire to become a professional handball player I would have just transferred to another club with a better trainer, but I didn't, I quit. This became one of the greatest life lessons for me, and to this very day I always reflect upon this time to remind myself to make sure that I only do things which I have a burning desire for or I will not do it at all.

At the age of 20 I took the next big step outside my comfort zone. I was looking into a military officer program because leadership had always been such a big strong point and interest of mine. I completed all the of the required entry tests and I received some really great scores. However, I did not choose to continue with it and instead chose to follow my older brother's path and study IT just as he had done seven years earlier.

The student life was fantastic! I really enjoyed my time at university, studying information systems. I never had to worry about anything. I spent my time studying during the day and working as a bartender or partying at night. It really was loads of fun however, not very meaningful at the same time. After three years of having no real purpose, I became bored.

I wanted to do something more meaningful in my life, so I started to search for new options. To interact with lifeless objects all day such as computers wasn't the lifestyle I wanted. I loved working with people and I knew that this was the new direction I wanted to take, as connecting with people left me feeling so much more fulfilled something that working with computers could never do for me. I discovered the role as a project leader and decided to take courses in that because I felt it was more suited to me. I didn't know it back then, but this was actually the first small step I took which would lead me to my life's purpose. Today I live by this. It is my vision to inspire and help people to achieve what truly matters to them.

After having this revelation about my life's purpose, I decided to explore other possibilities in Australia as an exchange student because I have always had an adventurous spirit. I became active in Australian business forums as I wondered if it would be possible to start my own business when I moved. I received one response from a lady who claimed to have something that may be of interest to me. Obviously, I didn't know her and as a human we want to know, trust and like the person we listen to so she added me on Facebook and began talking to me about a new business opportunity in Australia. We then connected on Skye where she showed me a proper presentation about the business. This was the first time I was exposed to network marketing.

At first I was not impressed by the presentation and began to swipe my mouse over the 'hang up' button after 20 minutes, but then something from the back of my mind reminded me of my current lifestyle and the lack of meaningful future I had, so I persisted with the presentation. From this little decision came a great outcome. This was ultimately one of the most important decisions I made in transforming the rest of my life and determining the person I would become.

I decided to join the company on the 1st of May 2014. From this very moment a whole new world which I did not know even existed opened up to me. Suddenly, I found myself spending all of my time watching personal development videos on YouTube all day. I got so addicted (that's right, addicted!) to all of these personal development videos which the company had shown me. I was even fortunate enough to have 'one on one' time with the inspiring leaders of the company as they taught me some valuable lessons on how to succeed in life. For me, this was so empowering as it gave me a taste of what life could be like. The attention and welcoming attitude from everyone filled me with happiness. I had been completely hooked in a whole new way that I had never experienced before.

The more time I spent attending seminars around the world and researching personal development, the more my life started to improve. Just after one year I started to see the significant impact it had on what I achieved and accomplished. I even noticed my personality changing as I began to expand my view on life. I learned a lot about how to communicate with people effectively when I read my second personal development book called 'How to win friends and influence people' by Dale Carnegie. At about the same time I had a struggling relationship which had just ended. However, when I applied the skills which I had gained through this book, I was able to rekindle the relationship and a week later we were a very happy couple. Ultimately, this made me start to realise just how important personal development really is!

About a month later the company announced another seminar which would be held in Bali for five days specializing in leadership. This was a very exclusive event as it was limited to only 200 people. This meant that everyone would have the privilege to work very closely with the director of the training which was quite an honour. As I discussed earlier, leading people had always been a great passion of mine so this was my chance to really go for it and develop those leadership skills. I booked it right away! I had the money so why not, right? One month earlier I hesitated to invest $ 200 on training with the travel and accommodation costs included, now I had already invested $ 3000+ on training, travel and accommodation.

Notice that I don't use the word "spend" because I see it as an investment. It is very important for you to see the difference. Self improvement is never an expense, it is always an investment!

It's the 20th of July 2014, I'm boarding the plane to Australia with one of my best friends for our exchange student semester. For him this would be a whole new adventure, but for me it was more that just an adventure, it was going to be a life changer. This was just one of the twelve flights I was going to take in next five months, travelling to different seminars around the globe.

As you can guess, these five days at this leadership development program were full of priceless information about understanding how to communicate with and inspire other people through leadership. Now I am able to pass on my knowledge around the world through my coaching. But right now I wish to personally share with you the two most outstanding skills which I learned from this seminar. I don't exaggerating when I'm saying that this two things could change your whole life.

Firstly, being able to determine what personality type you and others are is the key to effective communication. Ultimately, we categorize people into

four different groups (each being represented by either red, blue, yellow or green). People that fall into the 'red' category are typically very focused on their own needs and are very driven by success. Hence, they are also money oriented. Adventurous and spontaneous people are classified as 'blue', they crave all things fun! 'Green' best represents logical thinkers where they analyse everything that happens around them rather than act spontaneously like those in the 'blue' category.
Lastly, the 'yellow' group symbolizes selfless people, as the prefer to do everything through helping or being nice to other people. They also have a tendency to love animals.

When we understand how the different personality types respond to the world we are better equipped to inspire and help them effectively. For example, if you are about to sell a product to a yellow person when you yourself are a red person, you might only talk about how this product will help them make more money. This will be an ineffective selling tactic as yellow people don't correspond to that. Whereas, if you were to talk about the benefits this product would have to other people, it would dramatically increase your sale chances. Similarly, when it comes to inspiring people you must be able to establish a connection first in order to assure them that you are able to help them. The key is not just having the information, it's to take action from it!

The second most important skill I gained from this experience was the value of visualisation and habit. Ultimately, everything had led to this final piece of crucial knowledge, It was to write down our goals for our future and visualize them to the best of our ability. The whole process took about 2-3 hours so it was not just something you could complete whilst watching tv, it required a 100% dedication. We were instructed to write down a goal/affirmation for each specific area of our life on small pieces of cardboard. These became what we call goal cards. Since that day I have read them each and every morning before I get up in the morning and before I fall asleep each night.

The key to this process is to attach feelings to your visualisations as the more you truly believe in something, the more likely it is to actually happen. I ask you now to take a moment to look around you at all the manmade objects before you, it may be as simple as a pen or computer. Now think about how they were created. What do they all have in common? Thought. Each and everyone of these objects started as a thought in someone's mind before they became a reality. Back then I underestimated the power of this technique and how big of an impact it would have on my life. Today, I can see the results unfold right in front of me.

This now brings me back to how I began this chapter, when I was being faced with the worst moment of my life... With all of this valuable knowledge from four big seminars and hours and hours of personal development training online, I was able to snap myself out from my dark frame of mind. It is amazing how our brain can find solutions in almost anything when we really take the time to focus purely on finding a solution rather than dwelling on the problem. Worrying about a situation will only cloud your judgment and make matters worse. I told myself that I was going to survive this. I knew I couldn't wait any longer to get a job and work for two weeks before I got a salary so I desperately searched for an immediate solution.

I decided to try the bank options again, only this time I was going to have to take whatever I could get. This went against all of my principles because I had been raised to avoid unreasonable loans at all costs, but I desperately needed an immediate solution. So I looked at all of the banks I had ignored previously even though everything in my head was screaming at me to not associate myself with such banks.

I was unpleasantly surprised to discover that not even these banks would help me with a loan, even though I would have made them a fortune with the ridiculous interest rates they had! However, it did make sense considering I had absolutely no security or stable income. I was just naive enough to believe that I could get a loan just by paying more for it. Still I refused to give up and after a few days of searching for ways to get a loan I found a bank that offered to help me. As they could see my desperate attempts with other banks they decided to take advantage of my situation and offered me a horrific deal over a 15 years period. I understood what a terrible deal this was but I had no choice but to take it.

When my application had officially been approved and the money had finally been transferred into my account I did not feel happy, rather I felt incredibly relieved. A great burden had been lifted from my shoulders, for now at least.. With $ 10 000 in my account I rushed to pay off all my unpaid bills as I hate owing people money. Then suddenly at long last, all of my chronic stressing had been resolved. I was able to live comfortably again.

With a lot of money remaining from my loan I could now afford to go home to Sweden and continue study or work. However, if I am to be completely honest the only thing that was attracting me back to Sweden was my ex girlfriend. We had "paused" our relationship since I was going to Australia but we still had strong feelings for each other. So I contacted her and asked if she wanted me to come back and live with her in her apartment. The answer I got confirmed that I had nothing to come back to in Sweden.

In that moment I started to realise that everything was aligned for my career. I had been working towards becoming an international public speaker, which is my ultimate goal. I lived in Australia which I believe is such an amazing country because of the wonderful people and lovely weather. I had a ticket to a personal development event in Thailand in December, plus the flight there and back to Melbourne already payed. So without anyone who really cared about me in Sweden and enough money to last a fairly long time, I decided to start over from scratch. And so my new life began here in Australia. It was here that I would create the home for myself that I always wanted and bring my vision to inspire and help people to life.

However, like with all major decisions this did bring some challenges. Firstly, I needed to get a new visa so I could stay longer in Australia. I also needed to find a new apartment and get a job. Fortunately, it didn't take me long to find a nice, fresh student apartment that I could have until the new year in Brisbane. It didn't take long after that, that I found myself sitting on another plane travelling from Melbourne to Brisbane, ready to restart my life. It truly was such an incredible feeling to have broken all the social norms and just go for it on my own. In fact, that's one of the most important pieces of advice I give to my clients, that life is all about taking your own path and not listening to the people around you who don't have the courage to go for their dreams.

Between Christmas and new year I started to realise that I need a job really soon as my money was beginning to run low again. I also needed to find a new place to live by the new year but couldn't afford the bond for most places and only had enough money for about a months rent. So I decided to move into another hostel since you do not have to pay bond there and just pay by the week.

Just before I was about to move to the hostel I called an old Swedish friend that was also living in Brisbane at the time. I asked her if she could help me move in which she happily accepted. Not only that, but she asked me if I wanted to stay at her place for a couple of weeks until I found my own place instead.

I said yes right away! at this point I was so low on money that she was the only one who was able to buy food for the both of us. After about two weeks of sitting on the sofa looking for jobs I finally got a phone call from a person named Brad. He had read my cover letter for a position as a coach and loved my passion to inspire people. He offered me a job as an independent coach, using their materials. However, to be represented as one of their coaches I would have to of paid a lot of money for training which was quite a stretch for someone in my position! But I knew this was an amazing opportunity which could fulfil my dream to become an international public speaker. So I accepted on the condition that I could have some more time before I started in order to earn some money to be able to pay for the training.

Almost immediately after this wonderful phone call I received another one from a removalist company that had offered me a job. As if this wasn't enough, my new boss also had a room which he was wanting to rent out so I took it. I couldn't believe that in just one phone call I had gained a job and a somewhere to live. I was so appreciative.

After a few weeks of finally working I started to look into the public speaking/coach job again,
as I now had enough money to start up my own business and follow my dream. At this time I wrote down some new goals I wanted to achieve for the next phase of my life. One said "to live in my own lovely apartment" whilst another said "to have a wonderful girlfriend". So I added these goals into my daily visualization routine.

It would take me another three months before I could afford to move out from my boss's house into my own apartment and begin my coaching. It proved to be well worth the wait! I eventually found a beautiful apartment close to the city but unfortunately it was way too expensive to live there by myself. So I found a girl on flatmates that wanted to share the apartment with me. Finally, I now had a place that I could call home for real, first time in ten months. Not only that, but the girl I moved in with was going to turn out to be my girlfriend.

Our home is now filled with our goals and visions which we acknowledge each and everyday. We have a whole wall just dedicated to our goals! Now a normal routine for me is to read my goals cards and visualize them as though I'm already living that life or have achieved that accomplishment. Additionally, I have my vision board hanging in the bathroom which is full of pictures of famous public speakers.

There are also more specific goals hanging in our bedroom about my coaching as it is important to recognise all the little milestones you have to achieve before you are able to reach your ultimate goal. It's even extremely important to break down your milestones into microsteps which you can take every day in order to constantly maintain focussed on your goals. Since we always carry around our phones I also have my vision board as a background as it is all about getting exposed to your goals as many times in a day as possible.

Having just reflected on my journey so far here in Australia, I can honestly say that I am finally living the lifestyle I had created in my mind through visualization six months ago. Going from having no one that cared about me or not knowing where to live or having no money to eat a proper meal, to having someone that really cares about me for the first in a long time and to have a lovely home with healthy food on the table, has made me feel so incredibly blessed. However, the best part is what makes me feel fulfilled. That is the chance to inspire and help other people to use their mind to shape their world as they want it to be.

I could never image how fast great things would come to me! Right now everything seems to be going my way with new opportunities coming in each and every day. I am also fortunate enough to be able to surround myself with great people that inspire me.

I am still continuing to use all of my personal development skills, however I am now choosing to use them for teaching purposes so that I can help more people. Remember it is so important that we gave back, as life is about giving not taking. We can only reach a true sense of fulfilled when we help other people. This is because the chemical, kemical oxytocin is released into our brain when we help others which creates this feeling of fulfilment.

I want to finish off this chapter by saying that you can achieve almost anything if you have a burning desire for it. I worked my way up right from the very bottom, so if I can do it so can you! You can either have results or excuses, but you can't have both. Additionally, never listen to those who do not believe in your goals, instead surround yourself with people who are like minded and live a lifestyle which you desire.

Find a mentor to follow! Create a habit to always read or listen to some kind of personal development every day for at least 15 minutes. Most importantly, use the power of visualization! Imagine yourself being the best possible version of yourself or achieving that lifelong goal of yours. The more feelings you put into it, the more real and powerful it will be for your subconscious mind. Overall, I hope that I have inspired you to take action with your own life and appreciate it. You always have a choice when it comes to the life you live even in dark times, so make it extraordinary and don't waste a single moment! I believe in you.

Ted Gunnarsson

About the author

Ted Gunnarsson was born in 1992.

He grew up on the south east of Sweden in a village called Högsby where the population was as little as 2000 people. His mother Laila is a dental assistant whilst his father Christer works as truck driver.

Unfortunately, the couple decided to part ways when Gunnarsson was four years old. He also grew up with two older brothers whom are five and seven years older than him. The family stills remains in close contact.

Today Gunnarsson is living in Brisbane with his Australian girlfriend. He is working as a public speaker around the world conducting workshops and seminars whilst coaching with a company called YB12.

Through his mind-set and strategies Gunnarsson is inspiring people to have the best year of their life.

Teds Facebook page

http://tiny.cc/Ted-Gunnarsson

Developing a successful mindset

It's amusing how small things can make big differences when you are very young. I was only 5 when my family moved from Adelaide to Sydney. As the Adelaide and Sydney education systems are slightly different, the schooling year levels don't quite match up. Subsequently, I started school at a year level where school mates were generally about a year older. A 12 month age gap doesn't sound like much - yet when you're 5 years old that means your peers have had 15-20% more life experience. That one year's gap made a huge impression on the development of my self-perception of academic ability and overall competence. Seeds were planted of incompetence that I carried for years to come. Although so young, I distinctively remember teacher directives being blurry and not being able to connect the dots of instructions. Because of this difficulty, I believed that a level of difficulty and hardship was to be my portion for the rest of my life! That year I finished in the bottom three of my class.

Because of this internal framework I had built for myself, after returning to Adelaide at age 7 I acted out a lot. There was a place at my school called 'the thinking room' where I spent every other day...it was detention. My philosophy throughout my younger school years was 'respect is earned and not given' and this mindset definitely didn't go down too well as a 10 year old towards his teachers!

By 15, through church influence, I had more or less settled down when in the most horrible of situations, life threw the very worst of curve balls out of nowhere: my mother had a seizure and we found out she had developed brain cancer. With the cancer inoperable, over the next year she deteriorated from a bright articulate woman who did everything for the family to us having to take care of her. During this period my dad was a rock. My mum was my greatest advocate and the courage and dignity she possessed was inspirational. She passed away when I was 16.

By the end of school I was very sensitive to the question, 'what are you doing after school?' I had no idea! I made sure I did enough to pass my exams. I figured if you invest 14 years of your life into something you may as well pass. Yet with no goals to shoot for, or mark to inspire to, it's a safe bet that I didn't set any records with my exam scores! I believe you can really only achieve what you aspire to achieve – one without aspiration is one without achievement. Scottish philosopher Thomas Carlyle said "A man (or woman) without a goal is like a ship without a rudder".

Interestingly, although I had no University score to aspire to it wasn't the be-all and end-all that I thought (or was perhaps was taught) that it would be. I since found out that Albert Einstein hated school and failed to complete his schooling – and even failed a special exam to get him into college. Other drop- outs include Ronald Reagan, the Wright brothers, and Richard Branson.

At a cross-road, and probably still carrying a little bit of my formative year's rebellious streak, I decided to break the mould. Not finding the prospect of following convention and studying at University for several years or joining the 9 – 5 rat race attractive, I decided to start my own business.
Having received a casual job in car cleaning through my brother in year 12 it was my only real job experience and industry to draw on. Additionally, I had no money, and lacked the self-belief to get a business loan if that were even a viable option. Despite this, I was excited in that I believed I had discovered a niche market in car cleaning that could work well. With only my pride to lose I went out and bought a $30 hose and a $20 car cleaning chamois and explored the market-gap. It was a great hit from the start – with business taking off through word-of -mouth referral and without the need for any marketing or advertising.
I discovered the power of customer service and learning client's personal names in relationship building. I believe one of the best ways to grow a start-up is to see what normal expectation in an industry and perform above and beyond. By over performing rather than over selling you develop what I call a 'grace bank': room for honest mistakes or genuine mishaps should they occur - with customer appreciation that soars.
Within a few short years I along with help from different friends over the years found myself as the owner of one of the largest mobile car cleaning businesses in the state – cleaning over 700 vehicles per week with dozens of cooperate clients...all on an overhead of just a couple of hundred dollars per year.
This was all very exciting, but also a tremendous learning and incredibly changing time.
The world of business self start-up is stretching. You get pulled emotionally, financially, and spiritually. It can be like a giant mirror, where every short-coming, criticism and weakness stares you in the face. Businesses often

have the founders DNA in them and be are often an extensions of one's self. The challenge is therefore broadened from not just the business world but in personal life as well. This applies to all pursuits where we leave the comfort zone to embrace the risk zone, you will find yourself in an amazing accelerator for personal development.

I found myself praying often and great answers would came, though not always in what I would call my perfect timing. But after the early roadblocks my faith in life was growing and I began to operate in belief. To me, hope needs to join hands with belief because hope is passive and belief is pro-active. At one car dealership I was contracted by, a mechanic called Larry was complaining to me about severe back problems and that he had seen several chiropractors and would very soon have to go to another. I offered to pray for him and he agreed. Placing my hand on his back we said a simple prayer. About a week later Larry called out to me from the other side of the yard. He was grinning ear to ear and informed me he had not had the slightest of back problems – he had been healed! I then preceded to witness a grown man in his 40's do a chicken dance right there in the public! He did twists and turns and squats and you name it! This was a great learning experience to me that great things can be possible for those who step out and believe.

Life became my teacher in business. At the beginning, with no formal business experience or education and quite young, I had no clue as to many things! I would be asked for things such as a remittance slip with no idea what one was. Thank goodness for Google! In a way, I followed the old adage of 'fake it until you make it'.

This concept is not about being fraudulent but convincing your self conscious self of certain truths and then acting accordingly. There is much written on 'The Law of Attraction' and it is certainly worth exploring. What I do know is everything that exists or is a current reality first began as a thought or conception. Positive thoughts leads to positive actions which leads to positive results. Before you know it you are surrounded by positive people and a reality has been manifested by simply believing it. One of my favourite quotes comes from Henry Ford who said 'Either you think you can or you think you can't and in both instances you are right".

Early on I hated cold calling and approaching new clients. It made me feel ill inside and fear prevented me many times from growing my business. This was a fear of failure, embarrassment, and simply approaching managers in fancy suits. Over time I learnt that it was very helpful to simply calm down and not be so emotional. Sometimes emotional detachment can be very useful. I would sit in my car before approaching a client and say to myself, "it's 11:30 am, by 11:40 am I will be sitting in this car again. The radio will still be playing songs and I'll still be breathing. If the answer is 'yes' then I have made thousands of dollars in extra revenue. If the answer is 'maybe' then I have gotten good exposure and potentially a new client. If the answer is 'no' then I can rest in the knowledge and be proud that I did my best...which is all you can do. It will simply be 11:40 am instead of 11:30 am".

Matt Damon said it well in the 2011 movie, 'We Bought a Zoo': "sometimes all you need is twenty seconds of insane courage. Just literally just twenty seconds of embarrassing bravery. And I promise you, something great will come of it".

I suggest writing down the most audacious and far-out there goal you have and acting upon it. Do something you have no right doing and make it your right. When we confront our biggest fear all our other fears shrink into near nothing and we are empowered over them.

A car dealership owner friend of mine who didn't particularly enjoy approaching customers found himself sitting in a pub opposite Mick Jagger and his entourage. My friends group dared him to say hello to Mick. He gathered his courage, approached Mick and offered to buy him a beer. In short the rest of the night was spent drinking and partying with Mick Jagger who left him a note calling him 'his good friend'. Do you think my friend had any trouble approaching customers after that? Even if Mick had not been so hospitable, when you face your greatest fear every other fear become easy and even if you come up short you'll still be far ahead.

Eventually I got married to my wife Melissa, who is my greatest supporter. Wanting to take my business to the next level, I brought on a close and old school friend whom I had known since we were 9 year olds as a business partner. He said all the right things, but unfortunately, words and actions are very different things. The business simply stagnated.

I believe idealism without implementation is procrastination and prescribe to the Nike slogan of 'Just Do It". The "make it happen' mantra can be a struggling entrepreneurs salvation as no-one else will do it for you.

With my new partner we didn't go backwards but didn't grow either, and I was all about growth. If you're not growing you are actually dying, and in business and life we need to be like a hermit crab who moves to a bigger shell when outgrowing the current shell. Sometimes we out-grow people around us which can be very painful and some relationships may be meant for just a season. In the change-over between shells, you are vulnerable and exposed as the hermit crab, but if you don't make the move your spirit (old shell) can get crushed.

In addition to growing, self-promotion should not come by comparing yourself to others. Comparison leads to a forked road and both outcomes are bad: either you out-do your competitor and fall into arrogant and unattractive pride, or, you come up short and fall into an inferior complex. Set your own dreams and run your own race to the tune of your own expectations.

After a period I would notice little amounts of money began to disappear from myself and my partner's joint business bank account here and there without explanation. Communication with my partner got more and more sporadic until his phone voice mail would send chills down my spine. After a period my friend confessed he had issues with drinking. Very large sums of money went missing until eventually, I would learn he was a full-blown alcoholic.

Throughout this period I was stretched between loyalty and support to my closest friend and the insistence they receive the professional help they would not get. I was utterly torn and haunted by the questions, 'what is the difference between being supportive and enabling addiction?' 'At what point are you funding a damaging lifestyle or pulling income from someone with a sickness?' In the end the situation become untenable and I made the excruciating decision to end the partnership. We haven't spoken since.

With this disappointment and feeling disenchantment with my business not being as scalable as I would have liked, in 2014 I made another leap of faith and launched another entrepreneurial venture with my business partner and close friend Dan Clarady. We decided to make a website that made booking and paying for home services in under 60 seconds possible. Working 12 hour days we bit the bullet and Bookah was born.

In need of finance, I decided to enter the world of commercial office cleaning. With no experience in the industry it was a bold move. I cold-called businesses with many rejections.

The problem with giving up is that you may turn over 99 stones but how will you ever know that under the 100th stone isn't the result that you are looking for? Leave no stone unturned! Finally an office told me they were not happy with their cleaners and asked if I could come in for a consultation. Dressing up with my best black shoes and shirt I printed up an Excel spreadsheet and picked up a clip board to look the part. At the office I was shown around the premises by management and would make random notes. Later on I realised the 'notes' were mostly random scribbles! After being shown around I was asked to provide a quote. This was a great problem as with no experience I had no idea how to price jobs. I didn't want to grossly over or under quote! Taking an opportunity to talk to a receptions I plainly asked her how much the old cleaners charged. She told me the figure and I was relived I had a number to work with. I added on 5% and scored a $25,000 a year contract.

A moment of truth for myself and Dan hit when we were invited to be screened for acceptance into the Entourage, a leading entrepreneurial teaching and mentorship income. Acceptance meant Dan and I sacrificing a sizable portion of our income to pay for the program to go along with interstate travel. It would have been so easy and safe to have said no, because we really couldn't afford it. But when opportunity presents itself sometimes you need to grab it with an iron grip. We felt we could create a scenario where we had no choice but to be successful.

I recall going on an introspective walk one day and seeing an old man emerge from his work place. Carrying a tired brief he sat on a bench. Slowly he pulled out a banana, peeled it and stared into space. The thought occurred to me, 'what if this man had done this every day for the past 50 years'? I wasn't judging him, for all I knew he probably loved his life, but the impression I got was that you only live once and choice is a large part of how our story will unfold. At that moment I knew that I could live with or without a lot of things, but one thing I couldn't live with was regret.

Dan and I invested into the program and personally and professionally we saw tremendous growth.
One of the best things you can ever invest in is yourself. It's fascinating to me how often millionaires lose their fortune in an economic collapse or for some other reason only to make it back by other means. Many lotto winners find themselves worse off a year later. The reason for this is because it is who we are, and the knowledge we possess that creates success. Business comes and goes and trends come ablaze and then snuff out, but investment in oneself carries on. We can save many years and much money off our own journeys by learning off others with been there and done that experience. It is interesting that if the world's wealth were distributed equally, there is a large probability, I believe, and that much of the wealth would wind up in the same hands. The reason for this is simple: Individual mindset and habits create outcomes.

My and Dan's investment has led to some great doors opening for Bookah. Our website www.bookah.com.au has now won national awards and we are partnering with billion dollar companies. Many angel investors are presenting themselves and the general response has been amazing.

For me, lauding the example of my mother, life isn't about what happens to you but how you choose to respond. Life somewhere is always more difficult for someone else, so say a prayer, be the best you that you can be, and get moving!

Craig Merrett

About the author

Since founding his first company out of high school, Craig has been a serial entrepreneur who has featured in numerous national and international books and publications. After spending years studying the positive faith, mindset, and action connection, he has successfully married these insights into successful business practice and exploring triumphant personal growth. Craig passionately enjoys sharing his insights with others. From Adelaide, South Australia, Craig is a keen basketballer who loves the beach and spending time with his wife Melissa and pet Rhodesian ridge-back Coby.

Just Start

From a young age, I've always desired to make a difference within this world and ultimately leave behind some sort of positive legacy by which I can be fondly remembered for all the right reasons. Given my independent mindset and personality I have always challenged the status-quo. Even from a very young age I strongly believed that everyone has one shot at life and that only through doing "our own thing" (as opposed to blindly following convention), are we able to make the most of every single day and ultimately reach our full potential as human beings.

From starting my own digital agency Crowd Media HQ and growing it to a multimillionaire dollar enterprise in a short period of time, to now running a venture capital firm Emerge Investments, investing in start-ups all around Australia, you could say that I have already 'made it'. While I have achieved considerable milestones at a young age, the purpose of sharing my story with you is not to indulge in youthful braggadocio, but instead to recall the difficult, unexpected and ultimately liberating experiences I have encountered from childhood and most importantly how the lessons I gained from these experiences have led me to the fortunate position in which I find myself here today in mid-2015.

At the intersection of the relentless change in digital communications and the Australian Small-to-Medium Enterprise sector, lies Crowd Media HQ. Founded in late 2013, Crowd Media HQ is a digital marketing agency with the specific aim of helping SME's to harness the power of digital communications technology in transforming their customer engagement and ultimately their bottom-line performance. Rapid advances in digital technology are changing the way markets operate across the world as we speak, however many Australian businesses have been slow to adapt, a situation we'd like to turnaround, beginning with our own partners.

Running the digital agency has taught me many lessons. I have failed several times from poor decisions, I have been pushed over the edge a number of times. But deep down there is always something that tells you to keep going. Applying laser focus to your personal goals, taking concrete action towards achieving those goals however audacious they may seem and backing yourself with the belief that anything is possible.

Here are a few tips that I have learned along the way:

GETTING OFF THE GROUND
1. Get started now
You've probably had an idea locked away in your head for a few years, and now is always going to be the best time to get yourself going. If you're waiting for a sign or for some clearer indication that you should get your new venture off the ground, then this is it. There's never a better time to start than now.

2. Work out why you're doing it
If you're in it for the money, then a new business venture might not be for you. No matter how good your idea, the money won't start rolling in immediately, and you'll likely lose your motivation to keep working. You really need to be passionate about your idea. An idea that you can't stop thinking about or talking about and you in your heart feel it's the right thing to do.

3. Learn your subject matter
This one should be obvious, but make sure you're going into your business with a solid foundation of knowledge. Of course, the journey will be a learning experience on its own, but if you're not adequately prepared then you could be left floundering in the deep end, which is definitely not the best way to start a new project.

4. Find a mentor.
Your mentor shouldn't just be there to show you the ropes of the industry, but make sure they can offer you important moral support, too. They can offer you guidance in what you're doing, and also be a great person to bounce your ideas off. A mentor like this is going to give you the honest feedback you'll need to push ahead.

5. Practice

If you want to be good at anything in life, you need to dedicated sufficient time to practice again and again and again. Learn from mistakes and modify your techniques until you achieve the desired result.

6. Goal Setting

Set goals, break them down into smaller individual tasks and work hard to achieve those goals, no matter the obstacles which stand in your way. As the timeless business saying goes, "what gets measured gets done".

7. Take Action

Most important lesson is simply to take action once you know what goals you want to achieve. The best intentions in the world will lead nowhere unless you get moving today. "Just do it"!

8. Stay Focused

Life is full of distractions, even more so today in our hyper connected digital world where a wealth of information and entertainment is at our fingertips. But to achieve your goals and ultimately be successful, you need to focus on one thing at a time. Easier said than done, but it's absolutely vital to channel your energy where it's needed, when its needed.

9. Keep looking forward

You're going to have a few setbacks, that much is inevitable. And whilst it might feel awful at the time, don't let these concerns disillusion you from your goals. If this is an idea or a business you're truly enthusiastic about, then don't let these small stumbles lead to a great fall. No one said this was going to be easy!

10. Keep it balanced

You'll have to invest a great deal of time into your new business venture, but make sure it doesn't take over your whole life. It's important to take time away from work to focus on your other needs, and give yourself the chance to come back to work with fresh eyes and new ideas.

11. Don't sell, educate.

Even if selling your product is your end goal, educating your consumer and becoming a thought leader in your area is crucial to your success, particularly in the early days. You need to establish yourself as a credible source, and as someone out there to genuinely be helping the consumer.

12. If no one knows about you, you won't get ahead

Getting noticed is always difficult, but there are different strategies you can employ to make sure people know who you are. Social media and networking are great ways of putting yourself out there. Otherwise, you might be caught screaming into the void.

13. Get the right team together

It's important to have a great foundation team on the ground when you're getting started, but make sure they're there for the right reasons. If they're money-motivated, they probably won't be in it for the long run, so work to get people who have the same vision as you.

IN THE OFFICE

14. Give yourself time.

Overnight success stories are rarely, if ever, the whole truth. In the business world, an "overnight" success can take months or even years to pull off, and recognition isn't going to come immediately. This is a marathon, not a sprint.

15. Take it one task at a time.

Multitasking might seem like a good idea at the time, but the truth is, you'll be a lot more efficient if you stick to one thing at a time. Not only will you complete your jobs faster, but everything will be completed to a higher standard if you're investing all of your attention into one thing at a time.

16. Stick to your schedule

Before you start on your work for the day, make sure you have your day's timetable planned out. Everyone works differently, so it might take a while to find something that fits. Divide your work into what's important, what's urgent, and what's a combination of both to figure out what to prioritise.

17. Networking is key

It's a phrase you have probably heard dozens of times, but that doesn't make it any less important. Now that we're all so connected via social media, you can network with people all across the globe, giving you the best information to help you succeed.

18. Don't be too loyal.

If someone has lent you a hand at one point in your journey, it might be tempting to stay loyal to them, as a sign of good faith. But by doing this, you could really be cutting yourself off from a myriad of new, and better, opportunities. Knowing when it's time to jump ship is crucial to sustaining your business' future.

19. Learn to say no.

It's important to be accommodating and helpful in your everyday life, but if you're really aiming to get ahead in the business world, make sure you're prioritising yourself. Saying no to people's requests might seem hard at first, but it'll make all the difference in the long run.

20. Stay informed

The business world is ever changing, so it's important to keep your finger on the pulse of current events. Small changes in the outside world can have big effects on businesses, so make sure you're staying up to date with all of the new developments.

21. Don't forget your manners

Polite doesn't have to mean passive, and a kind gesture is always appreciated. When working in a stressful environment, kindness can go a long way to improving morale, and people are far more likely to respond to you if you are a genuinely kind person.

22. Know your finances

No matter how vision-oriented your business is, if you don't have the cash flow to sustain yourselves, you won't stay afloat. Having even a basic knowledge of finance and your accounts will mean you won't be caught out with any surprises from the finance side of things.

OUTSIDE THE OFFICE
23. Don't neglect your personal life.
The people who were with you before you started your venture are often going to be the ones who will stay beside you for a long while. Having someone to come home to at the end of a long day will really improve your emotional and mental health, and keep your head clear when you're going back in for another day at the office.

24. Develop a support system.
Business is a stressful endeavour and it does take up a lot of your time. Be aware that some people might not want to stick around when you're hard to get a hold of, but they're probably not the people you'd want in your life anyway. Have a strong support system of family, friends, mentors and advisors.

25. Take some time off.
If you're truly passionate about and idea, the chances are you're probably working on it almost 24/7. When you're feeling overwhelmed, take a step back, leave your work in the office for the weekend, and use this chance to recharge your batteries. This will give you time to re-think, re-strategise and move forward.

26. Keep it moving.
It can seem too easy to just spend all your focus on your work and neglect other facets of your life, but exercise will help you more than you might know. Not only will it stimulate endorphins and get you in a better frame of mind to work, but consider a boxing class if you have some post-work aggression you need to sweat out.

CHARACTER

27. Remember: You *are* the company.

If you make a mistake, own up to it. Accountability will make you a more reliable and trustworthy face of the company, and even if what you're owning up to isn't a great move forward for your business, people will know that you're not only accountable but also responsible.

28. Discipline

Discipline is the most basic ingredient for personal success, no matter your goals. If you want something to happen or you need something to be done, don't make any excuse just do it.

29. Authenticity and Integrity

If you're going to be investing such a huge amount of time, energy, and money into one thing, it's important to make sure that you are authentic about what you represent, and that you truly stand behind the product. The consumer will be able to tell if aren't genuine, and your business will suffer as a result. Make sure you're standing for a product or service you believe in.

30. Keep on fighting

The life of a businessperson is never easy, and you're going to face adversity at some stage. To survive, it's important you have the tenacity, strength, and willpower to keep on going, even when things start to get a bit rough. That kind of strength and dedication to your vision will pay off in the long run.

Judy Sahay

About the author

Judy is the Founder and Managing Director of Crowd Media HQ – Melbourne based social media agency giving organisations a strategic edge through unique digital media solutions. Crowd has successfully executed powerful social media campaigns for big corporations, delivering effective, end-to-end social media solutions, from strategy development and community management to creative marketing campaigns and beyond.

Judy has keen interest in the way businesses interact, communicate and share information with consumers. Through her work with corporate firms, she developed an understanding of the ability of media to influence people's purchasing decisions. With the impending growth of social media, Judy recognised a new wave of marketing innovation and embarked on extended project looking at aggregation and visualisation of data between brands and consumers.

Judy brings a depth of knowledge within the digital sector. She has on numerous occasions, presented to local governments, councils, chamber of commerce events, private businesses and SME groups to share her views on the changing digital landscape. She has also appeared in the Sydney Morning Herald, The Age, Business Review Australia and contributed to a number of influential blogs and forums to educate Australian SMEs on the current trends within the digital landscape.

In 2014 she co-founded Emerge Investments, a firm that invests marketing, business and IT intelligence for start-ups and infancy stage businesses. She's currently on the board of several non-profits and start up businesses. Judy holds a Bachelor of Chemical Engineering, Bachelor of Science and Masters in Accounting/Business.

Apart from business, Judy devotes her time to family, friends, non-profit, community groups and youth groups. She is passionate about empowering young people to become better leaders, to create positive change and ultimately be in charge of their own destiny.

How losing weight changed my life

It's a phenomenon not many people would have experienced. You walk into a room and see a familiar face but that person has no idea who you are because you have lost so much weight you are unrecognisable. What started out as a determination to lose 10kgs of extra weight turned out to be a complete life detox, ending my marriage, and bringing me to the brink of losing my business and bankruptcy. The journey back has been a complete physical and mental transformation and my new life is indeed completely unrecognisable from the old.

I've recently turned 40, but my story starts in my teens when I met the man who would become my husband. I was at a birthday party about a year after I left school. He was best mates with one of my friend's older brothers and they'd set us up. He quickly started calling me and most days we'd meet for lunch, go for very long drives, or the movies. We ended up doing a lot together.

But I'd already planned to go overseas to study design and work in Milan. It was the days before Facebook, and mobiles were still really expensive, so while I was away we'd send faxes to each other and kept daily diaries. On the day I arrived back in Australia he'd filled my bedroom with red roses. There were dozens of them; all to show how much he missed me. "There were not enough roses to fill the room to show how much I missed you," he told me. We swapped diaries and read about our feeling for each other while we were apart. So instead of pursuing design in Italy I came home and married him.

We'd grown up from our late teens together, through the marriage. But when we became unhappy with our lives as individuals, it was hard for that dissatisfaction not to taint our feeling for each other. After being married for 13 years, he retrained into another career and that was the start of a difficult period in his life. Meanwhile I was becoming increasingly unhappy and gaining weight. I used food as a form of medication. It was easier to shove something into my mouth and suppress the emotion, rather than feeling empty and having to deal with it. So all it took was something negative to happen, a bad comment from someone, not having enough money, a terrible day at work or something not fitting me in a store and it was the trigger to eat. Expressing my feelings with food and yet feeling increasingly unhappy with my body was inevitably a strain on our relationship.

My list of comfort foods included the biggest bowl of pasta you'd ever seen with rich cream sauces, pepperoni pizza with extra cheese, hamburgers and chips or tiramisu, chocolate cake with cream or gelato. Sometimes I'd do a combination of all of the above. I might skip breakfast but gorge on an overfilled focaccia as a late lunch. If I needed a pick-me-up during the day I ate banana bread, telling myself if was healthy cause it was bread when I knew it was really just cake. I would start out feeling really hungry, or starving myself because I was upset, then I'd become so ravenous that I'd eat anything in sight and then some. Sometimes late at night I could eat an entire day's worth of food in one sitting.

It all changed one morning when I was getting ready to go to a networking function and the only pair of trousers that still fitted me popped the button on the waistband and the zipper broke. It was the loudest popping sound I'd ever heard. I sat on the bed and cried. And in that moment of abject misery I resolved not to be fat anymore. I decided I was going to lose this weight - forever.

I hadn't been overweight as a child or teenager, but in adulthood I had slowly stacked it on. I had attempted serious weight loss on two other occasions and had not only regained the weight that I had lost but also gained more on top. I'd become so wide I couldn't fit in the bathtub. When I took a plane ride I struggled to fit into an economy-class seat and had to request an extended seat belt. But probably the one thing that broke my heart the most was shopping for clothes. Some boutiques wouldn't even serve me because the shop assistants knew that the store did not carry anything that would fit me. Most occasions they would ignore me and look at me like I didn't exist - I was invisible to them. Sometimes I even heard them laugh or comment under their breath. If I did find something that I liked and asked if they had a bigger size, they would respond with "you're holding the largest size we have". I wanted to shrivel up and die every single time. I felt shamed.

Despite my tears, the day the button popped on my pants. I made it to the networking event and coincidentally there was a new member of the group: a personal trainer. I took that as a sign. I asked for his card and we organised a time to catch up. I admitted to him I was scared and I really needed help. I also told him that I'd do anything he'd ask me to do, as long as he helped me lose weight. At that point I weighed over 100kg. After we met and we started training together, he gave me some nutritional advice but suggested I also see a professional dietician. Two weeks later I was at the same regular networking meeting when I met a dietician. Again I took it as sign and made an appointment.

The dietician taught me that when times got tough, I'd need a carrot rather than a stick to motivate me because I was already so disciplined. I took his advice seriously and was aware that my 'carrot' had to be regularly reviewed as my lifestyle and short term weight goals changed. So the reward for each goal achieved kept changing but the only rule was it could not be food. At first, it was about being able to buy a new article of clothing. Although I was cautious with what I bought in the beginning because I was losing so much weight that I literally was shrinking out of my clothes. Some of those short term goals were taking regular bubble baths, buying a designer label leather jacket, taking a long weekend away, shouting dinner for my friends and weight loss support crew, buying my very first bikini, taking a plane trip without an extender seat belt. But the ultimate carrot was to have the body I had dreamed of while the smaller carrots helped me stick to the regime.

It was also the dietician who encouraged me to start visualising how the new and improved Stella would look. That's when I started sticking pictures up everywhere of my 'body crush' - Jennifer Lopez. That mental image really kept me going, especially when I felt I had nothing left.

I exercised with my trainer twice a week, at the start and end of the week, and the rest of the days was up to me. I was given a weekly training plan which I followed until we changed it every six weeks. I had options to change the type of exercise I did, but I still had to follow it religiously. Every Sunday morning I would weigh in and measure myself. I would then text my results to my trainer. I kept a daily food diary and I showed that to my trainer every Monday. I saw the dietician once a month to check-in on my progress .I basically followed this process over and over again in six-to-eight week cycles until I had lost the weight. The only changes I made were eating more food as my metabolism became faster and raising the level of training to make it tougher as I got fitter. There were only a few times where I stopped training completely and that was when I was really sick with a flu or started getting bored with the training. We'd have a break or do a physical activity that was fun like a hike or a walk run on the beach.

I also asked for the help of another person who was impartial and wasn't a close friend. I called them or met up for a coffee when times got tough. It was similar to the sponsor you'd have in a twelve-step program. After about six weeks into the new regime I noticed all of these emotions and thoughts were surfacing and I didn't have food as my comforter anymore. I had to deal with the bad feelings as they arose. Initially I was shopping irresponsibly, like buying a designer handbag for the price of a plane ticket overseas. Drinking was another way I coped when the food addiction stopped. Sometimes I'd drink so much I was barely able to stand and get myself home. But I soon realised both of these pastimes were no healthier than eating to excess. Eventually I started writing about my feelings and discovered it was the healthiest way to put them to rest. Keeping a journal was my way to heal.

My initial weight loss goal was to lose 10 kilograms – a task that seemed mammoth at the time. My husband was very supportive and enjoyed my weight loss. At the start I had gone through a phase of feeling really sick as my body underwent all the changes in diet and dealt with the new level of exercise. By the time I was down 20kg I had become an avid runner, cross fit trainer and had also started doing running events. That's when my husband started complaining that I was taking things too far and spending too much time exercising and not enough at home. He didn't want me to talk about training and weight loss anymore. As I lost more weight and started to socialise I became more confident in my appearance and what I was wearing. People started to notice the changes and commented, which was very uplifting. At this time he started to become a little possessive.

I had no idea how to deal with his feelings of abandonment and I reacted by shutting down. Just as he was having a difficult transition into a new career, I wasn't there to emotionally support him. From my perspective it felt like he was trying to sabotage my success . But in hindsight I suppose he was really just responding to me shutting him out. All I could do was close off and lose myself in my training. It became a form of therapy; one where I didn't need to speak about anything to anyone. I literally trained off my frustrations.

I lost 24kgs in the first eleven months and then another 12kgs in the following 10 months. The last 12 was by far the hardest. Most people are shocked at the amount of weight lost and others simply don't recognise me anymore. I find that I often need to re-introduce myself to people because my appearance has changed so radically. Their reaction was priceless and I took the look of confusion as a compliment. Of course everyone wanted to know the secret. But there was no trick or magic pill I took to lose all the weight. The challenge of sticking to my new regime was enormous. I would cry myself to sleep at night and wake up cursing in the morning because it was so cold I didn't want to get out of bed and train. It was hard but I never quit. I kept on going. I focused on the end result. I kept telling myself that the hard work it would take to remove the weight was nothing in comparison to how amazing my life would be once the weight was gone - for good.

I stopped listening and talking to people who were negative. At first the barrage of opinions about my weight loss was really uplifting, but after a while it became tiresome, especially when my husband and I were out together socially and all people wanted to talk about was my weight loss. For a while I even stopped going out socially until I was strong enough emotionally to cope with the attention.

But perhaps the biggest upheaval at this time was the end of my marriage. We had been slowly growing apart for years. There was no single event I could call the epiphany but my weight loss was, in hindsight, a breaking point. As the kilos melted away I was learning who I was as an individual, which was something that I had not been able to explore since being married. When I decided to leave it was one of the first times in my life, since I was single as a teenager that I acted on something deep down in my gut. My head and heart were in conflict with each other but my gut was saying "do it". I honestly thought I'd be gone for six months, just a hiatus, and then I'd return to my husband. But that wasn't the case. I didn't know what to expect at the end of the marriage nor did I even think I'd actually be able to walk away, so I just took a day at a time. It wasn't only me or my husband who was affected, our families were devastated and even our friendships were impacted – everything changed.

But the end of my marriage wasn't the only challenge I was confronting at that time. I actually didn't realise how bad my spending had become until I no longer had a second income from my husband to cushion my overheads and I was forced to cut up my credit cards. I realised later that I had been spending and buying things to mask my sadness. If something didn't fit me or I wanted something and couldn't have it, I'd become obsessive and just had to have it, no matter the cost. At times the spending was so bad that I'd choose a handbag or a new pair of shoes over a loan repayment or a utilities bill – it was out of control. When food was no longer my escape, I noticed how overwhelming my impulse to shop had become.

I saw the same spending patterns in a few of my wealthier friends who were also overweight. I noticed the high they'd receive from shopping. It was like a competitive sport for them, even going to the extremes of reserving a coveted item at an expensive boutique even before it was in stock. In the beginning it made me so jealous that they could have things that I couldn't and I wanted to compete. But after a while, as my weight started coming off, I realised how dysfunctional it was. Sure, I still like nice things and buy good quality items, but my heart no longer palpitates when I go shopping. If I don't have the money I simply don't buy anymore. I pay cash for everything now and only have a debit card. Once I removed that safety net another deep-seeded level of emotion around inadequacy and neediness surfaced. I had to deal with that too. In fact I challenged myself to see how well I could live on as little as possible. One of the goals I set myself at this time was to go on an overseas trip with just spending money, no credit cards. I recently did just that.

But with the weight gone, my solace from shopping removed and my marriage over, there was still another very large issue that had to be addressed. That was the loss of my design business. It had been my baby for ten years. My husband had worked in it and with the marriage over; he needed to extract his share. The debts and overheads had made it unsustainable. I was forced to close it, let go of my staff and sell off everything. I just wanted to go bankrupt and work for someone else, but my family stepped in. They came to me and said "we just want our Stella back, we don't care about the money we know you'll make it back 10 times over, but we don't want to see you lose 10 years of hard work. The business is yours. It's your name on the doorcalled Stella Design; it doesn't belong to anyone else."They fronted the money and encouraged me to build it again from scratch.

To make it succeed post GFC (Global Financial Crisis) I had to forget the traditional business methods of fixed workplaces and full time staff. Off shoring, crowd sourcing and cheap freelancing had killed the old design agency model. So I took the opportunity to reinvent the business and start it from ground zero by firstly replacing our full time team with contractors for scalability. We moved to serviced offices which enabled us to be able to work around the country and the world. This meant that we could develop an international profile and do global projects. We also embraced technology, using the cloud along with other electronic mediums to stay very learn while we scaled up. We started selling my personal expertise and I was able to branch out into speaking and blogging more than ever before. We got rid of all the excess overheads and kept everything super lean and efficient. My sister had grown up around the business and had already been working with me for a few years. So working together made us both hungrier for success. She chose to re-train from being a vet nurse into a social media expert and now manages the business with me full time. While it is very humbling starting all over again, it also means that you learn quickly from your mistakes and I can pick and choose who or what work I liked to do. At the end of the day a business should support your lifestyle and not the other way around.

There were times in my weight loss journey when I felt like giving up. When I was really stuck, and I mean feeling my absolute lowest in the world; feeling like a second class citizen. I would remember all the people who told me I couldn't lose weight and those who said I should stop doing all that training because I was so big and not built to do running or those types of exercises. Remembering how angry those people made me feel and being able to tap into that anger was the motivation to drive myself even harder.

There are so many things that I can now do that I couldn't do or even attempt before. I've run many distance events, including half marathons, mud runs and obstacle races. But it's not just those more extreme events that reflect the transformation. It's the more everyday things, which an overweight person can relate to, that are just as important to me. For instance, I can walk up a flight of stairs and don't feel like having a heart attack. I can stroll into any clothes boutique and pick up most things off the rack and receive pleasant service from shop assistants. Although I have to admit some stores I won't return to because my past experiences have scared me for life.

When I'm at home and I feel upset instead of eating I'll 'pattern interrupt' myself with a list of things I can do, to remove myself from the situation or feeling. I have some specific things I call 'side projects' that fall into this category. They're kind of like hobbies with ambitious goals. I've designed my side projects to be a reasonably big commitment, requiring a serious investment of time but have a conclusion that provide a sense of personal satisfaction. Some of my past side projects have included systematically selling off my old clothes on eBay, framing and hanging every piece of artwork I had collected, collecting and assembling the pieces to finish my Hello Kitty dolls' house, contacting one friend from my past each week, making a list of old movies I wanted to watch and then watching them, buying an old piece of furniture to restore, fixing it and then re-selling it, or making food like lasagne and cakes and giving them away to neighbours. When I ran out of my own side projects to do, I offered to do some of my friend's projects too.

If I'm out socially and I feel one of those old negative feelings emerging, I've learnt to moderate myself and the triggers that were once there, no longer have any power. I'm quite conscious of what I do and don't eat. I allow myself a cheat meal once a week only. But aside from that I don't use food as a reward at all.

Nothing could have prepared me for the knock-on affect my weight loss would have on the rest of my life. As a designer who specialises in branding, I now consider myself a living example of a life by design who has undergone a very major and successful rebranding. My exercise in self rebranding means the old Stella has changed beyond recognition.

Stella's 10 Point Self Rebranding Tips

My checklist for anyone contemplating losing weight or making a similarly big life change is:

1. Start with setting smaller goals that you can achieve on a daily basis. For example this week I am going to replace full cream milk in my coffee with skim or I'm going to walk every day for an hour. Keep it small and achievable.

2. Understand that your physical battle is a mirror image of the real issue – the mental battle. Be prepared to work on both or you won't succeed.

3. Work out your negative triggers before you start and have a strategy ready to deal with them. Hoping they won't happen is unrealistic. Be prepared because the triggers will come from places or people you won't expect.

4. Channel negative comments or responses from others into motivation. Find a way to transform negativity into something constructive. Don't take it out on yourself, on others and don't suppress the feeling either.

5. Changing the physical won't make you happy until you have learnt to love yourself. Be happy with who and where you are.

6. The greatest achievement won't be the physical change, but all the other new habits and actions that made the weight loss happen. It may be a cliché, but it really is the journey that counts.

7. Keep a journal. It's a remarkably powerful way to desensitise your emotions and take an honest look at your experiences and feelings.

8. Ask friends for help. Having go-to friends when you're feeling down is vital.

9. Always start with your end goal and use it when times get tough.

10. Visualise the new you. The more you do that the more real it gets.

Stella Gianotto
Founder and CEO
Stella Design

About the author

As Founder and Creative Director of Stella Design, I have lived and breathed the design industry for over 15 years. Considered a branding guru, I have worked with high-profile brands such as Sportsgirl, Sportscraft Group, SOCOG and Mattel, but have a soft spot for SMEs. I went out on my own ten years ago, frustrated with bureaucracy, high staff turnover and never receiving client feedback (as well as the boss looking down my top) and have never looked back. We do branding, graphic design, website design, and online development and eCommerce solutions.

Stella is my name and means 'star' in Italian. It is a universal mark of quality and excellence: everything our brand stands for. I'm constantly challenged to better myself and perform more efficiently and effectively for the benefit of my clients. It's so rewarding: from seeing staff achieve their goals to compliments from clients, I'm passionate about what I do. Success is rarely achieved alone – I have been involved with BNI, Italian Chamber of Commerce, Rise and Shine, AGDA and the Australian Web Industry Association.

Work is no longer work for me: I do it on holidays, late nights, weekends, even in the bath tub if I choose to. Now I have my own little empire – although small we are receiving awards and commendations. It's also about giving back – I guest lecture in design and mentor and nurture my creative team and interns. Outside of Stella Design, I enjoy cooking, running and participating in community events and fun runs.

Contact Details:
Stella Gianotto
Creative Director
Stella Design
P: 02 8217 0000
E: stella@stelladesign.com.au

A Classical Dancer in NYC Emerging Through Pain to a Life of Healing

When my doctor told me I would most likely have severe fibromyalgia for the rest of my life, I wish I knew then what I know now. That I would be able to go from sick and depressed to having a healthy body and a life full of joy. I now know how to see life through a unique lens that allows me to be aware of the limitless possibilities all around us, and how we can access vibrant health and happiness beyond what we've dreamed. We are powerful beings, and we can change anything in our lives. Do you have anything in your life you'd like to change or heal?

I auditioned for the performing arts program at Marymount Manhattan College in NYC and was admitted into their program on a dance scholarship. I was on my way to my dream career, where I would be able to perform on stage as a classically trained dancer. I moved to New York City to pursue my performing arts career just days before the terrorist attacks on the World Trade Center in NYC.

Shortly after beginning my intense dance program in NYC and experiencing the trauma of the attack on the city on 9/11, I developed chronic fatigue, chronic pain, and fibromyalgia. These challenging health issues put my dreams of a dancing career to an early end and forced me to really turn my focus inward to get healthy.

I remember the exact moment when I first realized that I was dealing with a health issue that would change my life. I had stepped out of my apartment and was walking to the corner to catch the uptown bus. When I finally reached the corner, I sat down and realized I was in so much pain that I had stopped three times to rest and take the weight off the pain in my feet. It was less than a block and I could barely handle the walk. I knew I was about to see my life drastically shift.

I started to make big changes in my life. I pulled out of the dance program before I even had the chance to finish the first semester. I started traveling around to different doctors and I found myself dealing with a new intense and consistent pain that I never anticipated I would experience.

I could almost always be found with ice packs on my feet or on my head. I was constantly trying to dull the intense pain and freezing my pain was a temporary help. To this day, even though I'm now healthy and no longer in pain, I find putting ice on my head so comforting that it helps me fall asleep.

As I went from doctor to doctor, it seemed that what I was dealing with could not be explained. I took at least a dozen different types of tests to try to find the origin of my pain and no one was able to understand why I was in such debilitating pain. That's when I was put on epileptic seizure medications, muscle relaxers and much more. I had a medicine cabinet full of pills and I was still hurting. I quickly realized that I was getting worse, not better.

Because I am such a sensitive person, an Empath, I was feeling all of the side effects of the medications. It seemed like the side effects from the medicines were a greater risk to my health and future, as compared to any potential benefits. All those chemicals in my body and the many side effects I was experiencing had such a negative impact on the way my body felt and functioned. I knew it was really hurting my body more than it was helping. I was depressed and the doctors were giving up on me one by one. I hit rock bottom. I was so sick at times that I felt like I was dying. I decided that the medications were definitely not the best way for me to recover.

Luckily I had an incredibly supportive family, and they encouraged me to look into alternative methods to heal instead of continuing to mask the symptoms with western medications.

Finally I went to the top diagnostic clinic in America, The Mayo Clinic. They confirmed again that my pain was real but that the debilitating pain would not end. They suggested physical therapy and bio-feedback to manage that pain. Their pain clinics opened my eyes to taking charge of my own health holistically, beyond traditional medicines.

I spent two weeks as an outpatient in a pain rehab clinic. Part of the treatment was a holistic approach to getting well, and I really gravitated towards this approach. My favorite holistic method there included the biofeedback machine to measure your brainwaves as you learned to relax your body and mind.

I started to seek Eastern, natural, methods of healing that didn't include medications or chemicals. We each have our own unique formula for healing ourselves, and I found daily energy treatments made an enormous difference. I combined daily energy healing treatments and herbal supplements with a change in my mindset and I started to see myself regaining balance. That was my formula for success and I started seeing big improvements faster than I had with the Western medicines.

I really put in the work, and I remember my herbalist telling me I was an excellent patient because I really followed his guidance! Many people say they want to heal but are not willing to do whatever it takes to get to their goal. My goal was to feel well and regain a healthy lifestyle once again. I was willing to do whatever it took to achieve that.

There was a little voice in my head all along that reminded me that I had choices in life, and even though the doctors told me "This is how it is," or "You'll always be medicated for these health issues," that little voice in my head reminded me that I could create something different. Now, as I look back, that phrase, "This is how it is" is my red flag reminder.

That phrase, whether you're telling yourself or someone else is saying it to you, is simply an indicator to me that they can't see possibilities ahead. It serves as a reminder that it's your job to look for the bigger picture and what choices you can make to create change. It does not mean it's the end, or that there is no choice like most people would conclude. We always have choices, even when it seems like we are *up against a brick wall* with nowhere to go. Let me be an example of that. I never stopped looking for ways to create change and create a life or body that worked for me. I didn't know what that looked like, but I never gave up. I knew something else was possible beyond what I was experiencing.

My mindset was a critical element of getting healthy. The way I changed my mindset was by beginning to shift away from being angry with my body for failing me, to being grateful for the parts of my body that were functioning well. What you put your focus on is what you create. So if you're constantly focused on your pain, you will be creating more pain. When you shift into gratitude for how your body is working, you are actually creating and attracting more of that.

I started to realize that thoughts are things, and that I truly had the ability to heal myself. At first the progress was slow, but it was the first time I started feeling any progress at all. I was encouraged and continued to work on healing myself holistically to create a healthy body and life once again.

SOMETHING BEAUTIFUL BLOSSOMED FROM MY HEALTH BATTLE

I didn't grow up seeing energy or having imaginary friends. My gift of clairvoyance, or clear seeing, opened up for me when I hit rock bottom with my health battles. That's when my extra abilities to heal and see energy naturally emerged.

While I was living in NY after the terrorist attacks on 9/11, I vividly remember starting to see energy in full color as if I was *looking through a new lens*. It first became obvious to me while I was on a bus or a train and I would see all of the energy around people and within them.

Imagine suddenly awakening to a new sense of sight that allowed you to see life in *technicolor*. I practiced by telling my friends what I was seeing and had them help me decipher what I was encountering. I could tell who was sick because their energy would be very dull, contracted energy. Alternatively, healthy people had vibrant, expanded, bright energy. I kept this new ability close, and only shared it with my most trusted family and friends.

As my ability to see energy rapidly increased, so did the skill of energy healing. One day while I was commuting home and had just stepped off the Long Island Railroad, I walked over to the bus to take me the rest of the way home. As I stood at the bus stop waiting for the next bus to arrive, I felt tingling start in the palms of my hands. There was a man next to me who started coughing and he looked rather sickly. The heat in my hands increased until I felt like there was almost a mini-fire in each of my palms. It didn't actually hurt, although it was very intense. Relying on my instincts, I just knew that there was energy coming out of my hands and going to this man who needed healing.

Similar situations like that kept happening where my palms heated up around sick people. Yet another sign, so I started to deeply investigate what I could do with this healing ability. I volunteered in a cancer center for years to get lots of practice with this hands-on energy healing, and the results I saw were always incredible. People told me how they not only felt more relaxed but how their health was changing from the sessions together.

I eventually learned how to turn my ability off and on so that I wasn't always bombarded with colors and spirits around me. Having the ability to turn it on and off like a light switch really helped me to continue to grow this gift instead of choosing to shut it down.

WHAT IS AN EMPATH?

Many of us look at it as a bad thing to be emotionally sensitive or to show vulnerability. We often feel emotional sensitivity is a weakness or just plain wrong; we try to push it down and cover it up. Can you relate? What if your emotional sensitivity was actually your greatest strength? Coming to the realization that *my ability to be incredibly empathic and emotionally sensitive* is truly a gift was one of my big *ah ha moments* that led me out of sickness and into health.

Have you ever been told that you're *too emotional*? Do you find yourself overeating or drinking a bit too much to cope with your emotional stress? Do you find that your feelings are easily hurt? Do you shut down when you're in big crowds? Is feeling *burnt out* a common reality for you? If a friend or family member is upset, do you start to feel it too? Do you need a lot of alone time to recuperate?

If you answered yes to most of these questions, it's very possible that you're an Empath. An Empath is a person who is capable of feeling the emotions of others, despite the fact that she is not actually going through the same situation. As an Empath, you will often take on the thoughts, feelings, sensations, and emotions of those around you with such intensity that they feel like your own. After watching a movie or reading a book that has an intense storyline, you'll feel affected by it for days.

As an Empath, you experience the world around you differently. You may often get easily *burnt out* or overwhelmed. Being empathic could also mean that you are constantly anxious about the possibility of picking up other people's problems, thoughts, feelings, or issues of any kind.

There are varying degrees of empathy and I fall into the extremely empathic category. I had no clue how to function with such extreme emotional and physical sensitivities, and I became an emotional sponge. I soaked up all the energy around me and I didn't know what to do with it. Eventually I became really sick, as I mentioned in the beginning.

I've spent over a decade developing my empathy, and learning how to use it as a gift instead of something that holds me back and slows me down. It has allowed me to not only create great health in my life but I also have created a thriving business empowering others who are highly sensitive individuals.

Some of the extremes I experience as an Empath include speaking with the spirits of people and animals who have crossed over. My sense of smell can be so heightened that I can smell bacteria in someone's body, and I can smell when someone is dying. I use my sensitivity to know when people are lying at any given moment. I am telepathic with my child and with the animals around me. I can see the energy fields of people and animals, and I use that information to determine where there are bodily imbalances.

Being highly empathic also allows me to be very tuned into what people require of me at all times, and I am able to connect on a deeper level with others at a faster pace because of this. Most Empaths are also natural healers, and I've used this gift of healing to channel energy to countless people with measurable results.

This awareness is positive in all the ways I've just described, but it's easy to take on other people's feelings and interpret them as our own. This can be quite painful for many Empaths, and I know it can be a huge source of suffering until you have the tools to empower yourself as an Empath.

NEW DEPTH IN MY LIFE AND CAREER AFTER HEALING

As I look back at how very sick I was, with a medicine cabinet full of strong prescriptions, I'm able to really appreciate how free I am within my life now. I haven't needed any Western medications for many years now. I no longer have any of the symptoms I once had to the shock of my doctors.

I healed a debilitating health battle that no one expected me to overcome. I realized it's possible to cure the incurable, and I'm grateful that I experienced this transformation because it has given me many gifts in my life. My own abilities as an Empath and Energy Healer emerged while struggling to climb my way out holistically from my extreme health challenges.

Although I have accumulated many credentials over the years, I feel my real credentials are overcoming the health crisis that was once so challenging and debilitating for me. Going through such extremes with my own health and emotions helps me to tap into what my clients and students are going through, using my own personal experience for perspective, and then I can relate empathically at an even deeper level because of my personal journey.

I'm no longer pursuing a professional dancing career, but my creativity is now channeled into my business where I can share my story and empower other people. You, too, can overcome your obstacles and find the peace and health in the life you deserve.

Don't let anyone fool you into thinking that you don't have choices. We always have choices and we have the power to change our lives if we are willing to seek out greater possibilities. What if your sensitivities and challenges were actually gifts and opportunities that could allow you to create a different possibility with your life? A slight change in your perspective could be what's required to start the healing and the change that you need to step into a life beyond what you ever imagined was possible.

Ashley Stamatinos

About the author

Ashley is the co-author of numerous #1 bestselling books, including The Energy of Expansion, and the Energy of Healing. She is widely known as the Empath Expert for her extensive work with highly sensitive adults and children. She has been interviewed on TV multiple times for her work with sensitive people. Her mission is to empower you to use your sensitivity as your greatest strength.

Ashley is the founder of Omorfi Healing, a business that she created as a platform to offer holistic education and healing to the world. She is passionate about teaching, and has been teaching for the last 10+ years. Within her practice she offers both online and in-person courses to those seeking a life they love.

While Ashley's main focus within her practice is supporting highly sensitive people, she also has many other courses available for you. She teaches on a variety of topics. Some of the courses she teaches include: The Mediumship Development Starter Kit; Stop Surviving and Start Thriving; A New Perspective on Parenting Intuitive Children; Empowering Holistic

Teachers; Ignite Your Holistic Practice; Seeing and Knowing The Bioenergetic Field; Empowering The Empath and Powering Up Empathic Kids, to list a few.

Wondering if you're an Empath? Take the free *Am I an Empath?* Quiz on the home page of Ashley's website. (See below).

Wondering if you have undiscovered Psychic skills? Take the free *What is My Psychic Gift?* Quiz on the home page of Ashley's website. (See below).

Private one-on-one phone sessions are also available for you. You can go to her website and click on Private Sessions to get all of the details.

Ashley travels to guest lecture and teach her specialty classes. If you'd like her to come to your business to teach a course or to give a guest lecture, please email info@omorfihealing.com for further information.

Get Social with Ashley:
Facebook.com/OmorfiHealing
YouTube.com/OmorfiHealing
Pinterest.com/OmorfiHealing

www.OmorfiHealing.com

Why I started out in business

Why I started out in business? Well. I guess the reason I started out in business was first discovering that I had a real interest for learning business back in high school. Studying and getting top marks, distinctions all across the board, my interest and knowledge in the subject really grew throughout that time. It directed my path of life towards business and entrepreneurship.

My interest in business really ignited during this time. The idea of making my own fortune and being my own boss. It all seemed like a way out from becoming what everyone else in my life was like at that time. I have been raised in council houses my whole life and, despite the countless hard times I've had, especially with the rough company you can find yourself in, I always fought against becoming like every person that I knew. I grew up seeing people that had, at least by my perspective, very little aspiration. People who would be unemployed and blame it on others, have some dull low-pay job or they clearly didn't enjoy or live a life complaining about price increases in supermarkets and on buses.

I didn't want to end up like that. Perhaps it sounds arrogant but life is so much more than petty whinging on about small amounts. The concept of business, the building of wealth and success through establishing an entity that can be much bigger than yourself, something you can be proud of starting and working for; That was the golden light to take me away from the life I've seen repeated so many times. That is something I would fight for everyday and still do to this day.

While my skills and knowledge grew, my aspirations has always been high. I am the kind of person who, were it to be in business, would never be happy with a simple dead-end shop on the corner of the street. I'll leave that to Arkwright! No, I want bigger, better. I want to stand beside the likes of these big companies we witness every day. More importantly though, I want to stand alone from the other companies I will be competing against. So when people see the business I have established, they wouldn't say "It's just another...company", they would say "Oh that's..." period.

I've had a few attempts at starting businesses in the past, all failures (Even after all the sales I've had). What was important though was that I recognised the mistakes I made and moved on stronger. My first step into entrepreneurship was a clothing company at 16/17 years old. The brand was called Predator. It was a brilliant idea in theory, selling tribal print clothing to schoolmates who would tell their friends outside of school and my plan for sales would grow the more it networks. I committed a business start-up taboo though in my Bambi-like state to the world of business; I didn't talk to the customer.

I simply went on to designing shirts and buying a copy of each to show people how good they were. When it happened though and I got the shirts, disaster! Too expensive, £10 shy of what school pupils would be willing to pay, no matter how amazing these shirts were. My start-up company flopped the very day it started. That was essentially £80 I had paid for the shirts wasted, but it taught me a valuable lesson to learn from and not a mistake I've made yet to this day!

Some readers out there will have also have noticed other flaws in my first start-up; the schools not allowing pupils to sell things, relying on others to expand/de-saturate my market and so on. These are more of the less obvious mistakes I had made but equally as important to learn from and progress. On top of this I would also have 'entrepreneurial spurts' when I saw the opportunity, such as selling out-of-date chewing gum to my classmates for cheap, but I feel none of this gave me any progress or development towards business. Merely demonstrating I had the aptitude for it.

It was on my 1st year placement at University that planted the seed for my latest (And most successful) business endeavour, Hire an Artist. In the last week of working at Brand Yorkshire, a Yorkshire based networking company, I discovered a canvas artwork placed just outside the office toilet. Looking at it and wanting a piece of art myself, the seed was planted. Some weeks later the idea grew and I made the decision to commission an artist for an idea that I wanted depicted in art.

When I couldn't find any company offering a straight-forward, simple and (Feelingly) secure and open-community style process, I spotted a gap in the market. And so the idea for Hire an Artist began.

I did months of research into the online art market trade, reading reports, journals, articles and blogs. Even listening to vlogs and commentary from key members of the online artistic community. My most involved research was attaining quantitative and qualitative information from over 50 artists directly, speaking with them and getting to know their personal lives as freelance artists.

After all my research I was confident that this was something that had great potential, something worth fighting for. Over time I had perfected my idea to maximise its potential and ensure it would be on the most successful path the moment I established it. It was at that point when I really gave myself the 'go ahead' and established my first officially registered company, Hire an Artist.

Early challenges I faced

As you'll probably already be aware with the life of the path of an entrepreneur, there are challenges around every corner. My life has been no different; if anything it's been far tougher considering my background, though I don't consider it a mitigating factor for failure in any sense.

My first early challenge was money; I was poor. You can start a company with just a laptop and a phone, in fact this was what I was doing, but inevitably you're going to need that one fundamental resource to life which is so notoriously difficult to attain. Money isn't something I've been greatly blessed with in life, our family's life didn't have good beginnings. It started with a mother starting again in life with nothing but a baby under each arm, my brother and myself, in a house that was so lacking it didn't have carpets for us to crawl on.

With that kind of background you need to fight especially hard for all of the doors (Opportunities) that have been locked as a result. My business required website development so advanced that 99% of web development companies wouldn't listen to me if my budget wasn't at least £10,000. I needed at least £10,000 just for the website, let alone the other involved costs, I only had 20% of that which was my own money.

I looked for ways for funding for a considerable amount of time. I made countless attempts including loans, grants, investors, angel investors, business partnerships and even crowd-funding like CrowdCube.com and Kickstarter.com. All had been failures. After all my attempts and setbacks I wondered why people weren't interested. This was clearly a golden idea and no-one was interested! Then I realised, I'm not an investable person; my second early challenge.

I was 19 years old. Still a business student. Little to no experience. No notable achievements. No useful family background. No credibility. I barely even had any online identity because I wasn't a sociable person; I'm highly introverted. I was a 'nobody'. The furthest thing from being investable as Hannibal was to vegetarianism! Why would anybody want to invest money in me?

I had no history of success behind me, no successful business endeavours, I was certainly no entrepreneur child prodigy. Inexperience was the most significant part of being not investable, not having that record of success to prove to people that I can make this current project a success was one more brick on the wall in the way of investment.

My next early challenge was family troubles. Considering that this is a chapter on the topic of entrepreneurship I haven't included the countless personal challenges I've had, though this one is particularly relevant because it involves barriers against your work. A close member of the family began to develop a mental illness and it really hit our family hard because it was so unexpected and no-one had any experience in dealing with it.

Because of this, I personally had to take time off from establishing my company so that I could focus on supporting the family. Not just supporting the person suffering with the illness but also the other struggling family members and even myself, as this kind of experience seriously takes a lot out of a person.

Now the reason I mentioned this as an early problem even though it's a more personal, emotional challenge, is because life can throw curveballs at you and somehow you need to prepare for it. It`s one example that I have where something completely unexpected, completely unavoidable can have a disastrous effect on your company. For me those dark days took 2 months away from me working on Hire an Artist.

A few months after this, when the business finally began taking shape, two more challenges become apparent; marketing and social networking skills.

For me, I'm young and fairly inexperienced to the world of business yet I'm already sensing marketing is simply not my forte. I'm an introvert and my verbal communication can turn pretty poor pretty quickly, that already is a setback to developing marketing skills let alone inexperience, considering that marketing is such an `outgoing, people-person` skill.

Lastly were my poor social networking skills, strange that I would be poor at this seeing as how I'm part of the first generations that grew up using social networks. There isn't a friend I know that didn't use Facebook in high school (Including Bebo and Myspace before the rise of Facebook). Twitter was also a big one but wasn't hugely apparent as Facebook sometime after Facebook. But nevertheless, while all my friends in school went nuts over it, I had barely even bothered with any social networking, which meant that, while everybody's online identity grew, mine barely developed whatsoever, as did my social networking skills.

So when it came to social networking for my company, all I knew was how to create an account and make posts! I didn't understand the value of likes/followers, I didn't know what kind of posts are the best, I didn't know all of the qualities that come into social networking such as engagement, shares, reach etc. After setting up my Facebook, Twitter, YouTube and

Instagram, I really struggled to use them effectively and still do to this day. Though I have made a lot of progress to developing my skills within this area which I'll discuss later!

So these were my early challenges; poor, inexperienced, not investable, family problems and weaknesses in marketing and social networking.

How they were overcome

Not to despair though, with every problem comes a solution. With clear thinking, a strong work ethic and relentless effort I overcame my challenges. Some of the toughest problems are now gladly behind me but some I still grapple with today.

The first early challenge I mentioned was being poor. So it's reasonable I talk about its solution first. As I said I needed at least £10,000 for the web development alone. The luck factor really came into play for this solution, as well as relentless effort and compromise. There was simply no way I could get the business I wanted in my current financial position and I couldn't get any funding because I simply wasn't investable. So I had to make decisions to have the company grow organically from one person (myself) and start from there, with no assisting staff. This was a compromise that would demand far more time and energy and would be challenging of my drive and work ethic, but nevertheless it had to be done to make it a company that could be established without investment.

Once I had done that I was left with company plans far smaller than they had originally been. Which was a website, acting as the e-business and the money generator, and myself doing all the work. A website and a person, that's all I needed in theory to start and run this business so that's the basis I went by. No marketing costs to ensure it gets sales, no workforce costs because I wouldn't take any money from it (until it was in the green). The fact was I just needed to get a business that works!

So the only thing I needed to pay for was a website. This wasn't a factor I couldn't compromise on though, any changes would cause big flaws. I still needed to find a web development company that would take on a project worth £10,000+ for £2,000, the most money I could personally invest into the company. And so my long journey to find my web developers began.

Over the time of 2 months in total I spent most of the day every day sat behind a laptop contacting web developers and web development companies, using all sorts of strategies. It actually doesn't sound too bad copy and pasting pre-written text into e-mails but over time it can really be highly tedious, and I came to highly despise web forms because they would always mean I couldn't always simply copy and paste a message like an email. Every day I would get rejections from the companies I knew could do it because my budget wasn't above £10,000+ and get acceptations from individual developers who on further discussion/research/analysis/case studies couldn't do it.

It was a really tough time and brought on indescribable mental fatigue and immense frustration but I kept my goal in mind and kept on going, this was something I wouldn't give up on. Eventually a company, Armer Design came to me who said they could do the project, some further discussions and they quoted me a little over my budget. After all the countless rejections this deal seemed too good to be true, I had explained everything clearly there was no misunderstandings, there had to be a catch. Cutting the story short I didn't accept to work with them until quite some time later, they were my only option, which was a good move because there was no catch! So that's how I beat my biggest challenges of being poor and not investable; a whole lot of hard work and luck.

Regarding the personal unexpected family problems, life's curveball, I both did and didn't overcome this challenge. By that I mean I lost because it took all my time and effort away from working on Hire an Artist and I never took it back, the storm went away and it's only then that I took time to work on the company again. In other words I lost because I waited for the problem to go away rather than beat it. I do consider it a victory at the same time though because it was at a time where it was very easy to take a lot of time off because of what happened, but I didn't do that. I got right back on the saddle and got back to work.

I mentioned that marketing was a big weakness, especially as I was unexperienced. This is one particular challenge that I'm still overcoming today. Had I written this a few days before I would have told you that I beat this challenge by taking on a marketing student as a potential business partner, that I replaced my weakness with a strength. Unfortunately he has dropped out because of other time commitments, an unexpected curveball but that's business and life!

But I didn't put all my eggs in one basket, placing my entire trust and dependence on another person, especially someone I barely knew. I've done particularly well to acquire some very useful connections beforehand. I'm getting experience in marketing every day and working with my connections and mentors to get priceless guidance and expertise. Marketing maybe my weakness but I've put myself in a very strong position to change that, in a sense I've almost overcome this challenge already.

Weak social networking was my last early challenge, another challenge that I'm still facing yet in the process of overcoming. I learned so much in a short span of time through experience and study, but mainly through experience. What I did was simply learn the value of each element in social networking; what it means to get a like/follow, a share/retweet, what the most engaging posts are etc. I then used what I learned and based my actions around them, what this translates to was consistent and regular posting and uploading good, interesting and creative content for people to see. This inevitably led to the 'Artist of the day' campaign which became a sure-fire method to guarantee fresh and original content daily, with plenty of other benefits that follow.

Where I am now

After more than a years' worth of work and challenges I now have a business, which will launch this year. I have a website that, despite all the hard times we've had from server shutdowns, development issues to hacking, has been professionally developed and can start earning money for the company. I have started a business from scratch!

As I write this I have a 130+ audience of artists and fans of art, 31 days into the Artist of the day campaign. I'm doing the work of two people, after my recent loss of a potential business partner after I took on more tasks for the company, and some huge challenges are still coming my way. I am in an incredibly demanding position of effort right now.

Some current challenges and weaknesses I'm facing involve trying to build a community, the obvious fact that I'm doing the work of two people, revising an accurate marketing plan, a lack of variety to marketing content, struggling for publicity, struggling acquiring more information direct from artists and devising an action plan for getting early adopters, of which I only have two projects guaranteed before I've marketed for the purpose of client projects. Just to elaborate and clarify what I mean by the last point, I'm already marketing towards getting artists and it's going well with over 100+ artists already interested however I haven't done any marketing towards getting clients and I only have 2 right now.

On top of this my future challenges involve a company with a child site operating under our name, competitor reactions (Which I expect will be weak as they themselves are weak competitors), the gargantuan amount of work that will be needed to run it successfully because of the sheer number of tasks required, getting enough client projects to match the number of artists that will be using the site, coping with the costs of marketing (If my planned future funding fails) and so many other challenges. That doesn't even count the problems I don't yet know about.

I'm far from disheartened though, I'm going to tackle my problems head on with a clear head, plans and a whole lot of work. I'm incredibly optimistic starting a business that could very well revolutionise the world of online art commissions. I even one second place in a Dragon's Den style business competition for £250. This is something I'm incredibly passionate about (Starting this company), it's actually one of the greatest jobs in the world and I'm not even getting paid yet (If you don't count prize winnings). I'm in a very good position now, with a business that *will* launch, not *may exist*, a supportive network of mentors and connections to give me guidance and expert advice for my problems. I have the ingredients for an artistic and creative community, the platforms for a good social networking campaign and actually in a good position to attract a new business partner.

So far I have fought hard and succeeded, honestly when I look back I'm surprised at what I've achieved both personally and for the company. There is far more hard work ahead and I've got more drive, more passion and more dedication than ever. I will succeed.

Advice to other entrepreneurs

The best advice I can give to you is to be like the phoenix. The ashes being your mistakes and perhaps even nothingness, nothingness in the sense you are creating something out of nothing. You will make mistakes in life both big and small, you can't avoid it. The life of an entrepreneur isn't easy, if you can't get up and dust yourself off after some mistakes, no matter how big, you're never going to be a successful entrepreneur. You need to arise high from your downfalls.

I told you of my frankly embarrassing rookie mistakes, of how I barely had nothing to start a company with. I didn't talk about this to outline how stupid I was, or how poor my beginnings were. I talked about this because it best represents my lowest of lows, or rather the toughest walls I needed to break. I talked about them to show that, prepare for cheesy phrase, I am the phoenix. No matter what life throws at me I will always get back up and come back stronger.

If you cannot harness some kind of attitude that resembles this you will fail on your first downfall.

My second best advice is to be like the hydra (Yes another mythical creature). Because you will face challenges in business, they can be easy or truly demanding of your efforts. I'm just an entrepreneurial youngster, I have so much still to learn, yet I'm already facing extremely tough challenges. But when it comes to brick wall problems though, problems you can't solve, such as what I faced with funding Hire an Artist, you have got to develop ways to get around them.

I call myself a fighter/survivor style entrepreneur because no matter what problems I face I will always tackle them. But I'm not foolish either, if I can see I'm facing a problem that I'm just not going to break, I find ways to get around them. In other words when one head is cut off I grow 2 back. My best example to this is trying to find funding for Hire an Artist.

I made countless attempts for funding, loans, partnerships, investments even crowdfunding, all had failed. I realised that I'm one of the furthest things from being investable. There was just no way I could have got the business I wanted in my current state. I didn't give up though. My original plans were cut off, the first head of the hydra. But I went back and fundamentally changed the way the business would be started, so it would be possible to start organically from myself. It was extremely costly, not by money but by effort, but it had to be done and it worked (Thankfully), the hydra grew back and came back stronger.

Also some 'sub-advice' involves creating a working sheet to share your ideas and thoughts, let people critique you! Including your idea if that's all it is at the time, don't keep it private thinking people will steal it, it's a common delusional belief with entrepreneurs and extremely costly. Putting your ideas on paper/screen/whiteboard helps you to remember your ideas, to share knowledge and ideas with others and so on.

Know your strengths and weaknesses, your threats and opportunities (SWOT analysis). Work on your weaknesses, play to your strengths, plan for the worst with your threats and how to beat them and take opportunities! I personally put mine on my working sheet which 3 people currently have access to, a Google docs sheet, because if they know my weaknesses they can possibly give advice on how best to beat them. I think this is just standard fundamental know-how with businesspeople though, I feel that I should simply remind you of this because it isn't always carried out in the best way!

This is the best advice I can give to an entrepreneur, as someone who is relatively new yet already fights big battles; become stronger from your mistakes, be a survivor, a fighter, know your weaknesses and look for ways around your brick walls. Do not give in; the life of an entrepreneur is an incredible one!

Gareth Craven

About the author

Gareth Craven, born 23rd October, 1994, is founder and managing director of Hire an Artist, an online art commission platform for people and artists to meet and create art. Gareth had appreciation for creativity from an early age, particularly from his late grandfather, Raymond who would regularly paint for personal enjoyment and share his works with family, some paintings of which have always been on the walls of Gareth's home.

Individuality has also been a prominent life interest with Gareth, who would strive to do things in his own way, such as unconventional celebrations; diving with sand tiger sharks with no cage for his 18th birthday. These interests, among many others, had fundamentally determined his path of life towards entrepreneurship.

Gareth first developed a passion for business whilst studying at High School where he had multiple entrepreneurial spurts alongside business studies. Using perfect developmental environments, in school he would sell anything from chewing gum to t-shirts, developing his skills and knowledge early on. A tactic used again in University, completing a six-week work placement with The Prince's Trust leading a 7 man team to fundraise for the charity, successfully raising £1,600 for disadvantaged young people.

Becoming a dedicated entrepreneur and business analyst, Gareth is currently studying in his 2nd year in Business Studies at Leeds Trinity University. Gareth is ambitious and committed to establishing a company that reflects his interest and values which can make a real change. His current and first officially registered company is Hire an Artist, which he hopes can revolutionise the online art commissions market.

Hire an Artist was first a small project alongside University work as far back as February 2014, reflecting his avid interest in creativity and individuality, until officially registered in late 2014, where it became to launch early 2015, located at www.hireanartist.co

How I created a six-figure start up business within 6 months of moving to a brand new country

It was the 19th March 2012. I landed in Australia with a 25 kg suitcase, a belly full of fear and excitement, and absolutely nothing else.

I was alone and I knew nobody. I didn't know how business in Australia went, and I definitely didn't know 'who was who in the zoo' here. I had no phone, no laptop, no job, nowhere to live, and no idea what the hell I was going to do.

Yet after just 18 months of rocking up frightened and blind, I had a business valued at millions of dollars.

Three years earlier, I had been in precisely the same position in Malta. On a whim, I had randomly packed up my life in the UK after a breakup. When I arrived in Malta, I was still extremely inexperienced in the world of business (especially in a foreign country, with another language). And yet within two months I had a contract with the European Government, a national bank, an international top-end hotel chain and several national retail outlets.

And there was a whole other journey before that...

Everything I have today in my profession and in business came from mastering how to create something from nothing, and how to overcome adversity.

I'd been working since I was 12 years old, and had volunteered in various educational roles before landing my first paid job as a 'welfare to work' Trainer. This was a UK national Government-funded organisation aimed at helping the long-term unemployed, ex-offenders and others to re-enter the world of work, education or training.

It wasn't easy applying for this job. I was still in university, and had no qualifications or paid industry work experience. I was considered too young, and incapable of doing the job. I had to beg, and promise to get an education degree if they'd take me on. But it paid off! I got the job (and surprisingly, without a restraining order attached)!

I was soon developing programs which would 'engage the disengaged', helping them move towards formal training and a sustainable career.

I loved the job, and discovered I was naturally very good at it!

Tens of my programs were being rolled out across the Southwest of the UK. My 'Work Steps Employability Program' alone resulted in 76% of long-term unemployed beneficiary claimants enrolling in formal training, or landing jobs for the first time in years!

It was so rewarding! Looking back on my life, I realised that even a 'rough-around-the-edges' gypsy girl like me could achieve monumental things on a personal level while changing other people's lives on a big scale. I had always considered myself an average nobody, just trying to get a job and carve out a career. But now I realised I was making a massive difference, changing the lives of individuals who were convinced that they couldn't achieve anything. Daily I heard my learners say, 'Thank you for caring,' 'Thank you for believing in me,' and 'Thank you for changing my life.'

I was making change happen. Good change, and I loved it!

By the age of 21 I had won an award in people development, and had been promoted to Training Manager for the Southwest of the UK. I very quickly went from writing work-readiness programmes myself to training others how to teach them. Now I was changing lives on a much larger scale.

I could clearly see the ripple effect of my work. Some call this the domino effect. I prefer to call it 'Efficacy Effecting'.

My passion to multiply efficacy had just begun!

An additional blessing was that I loved my manager as much as I loved my job. She was the perfect mentor for the wide-eyed, budding innovator who was committed to making a difference. She honoured my ideas and quietly applauded my achievements while giving me the freedom to create. Each time I stepped into the unknown, she watched with bated breath as I developed new programs – and together we waited to see what would happen. This contributed to the foundations needed to effect life-changing work, and was a valuable send-off to make an unprecedented difference in the world. I will always be grateful for her leadership.

Once accepted into university, I was catapulted to post graduate level qualification as a teacher in the adult education sector.

Everything was going fantastic! Until … One day as I skipped happily into work, excited for another day to begin, an ominous array of men in suits stood before me looking very, very serious. "Sarah," they said, "We're sorry, but the Government has changed; your contract has been declared redundant. You have no job."

I was stunned. I had just entered into a mortgage, and recently financed a car. My partner's father had suddenly passed away, and he had stopped working to care for his newly widowed mother. The timing couldn't have been worse.

But more than this, I thought about how many people still needed my help.

I thought of all the program participants who had seen dramatic changes in their lives. They had spread the word to others who were hungry for change in their own lives. I couldn't let these services come to a stop!

At first I cried. For days I forged ahead with my work, while quietly letting it all sink in. I couldn't let any grass grow under my feet while I figured it out. And I couldn't give up, but what was the next step? One thing was clear: I had to find other work, immediately. But that was easier said than done, because the Global Financial Crisis had just hit the UK.

I took a sober look at the new reality. I realised nothing had actually changed. Redundancy hadn't changed the fact that I still loved my work and I was good at it. Nor the fact that people still needed my help.

There was only one thing to do. Start a business.

Excited for the first time in days, I eagerly sketched my first business plan. Then came the naysayers. Mum told me to 'get my head out of the clouds, get married and have children like a good gypsy girl should'. My boyfriend, disgusted, told me 'don't come crying to me when it falls apart'. To face this opposition from the ones I loved most was devastating.

But I couldn't let it change anything. I knew what I had to do. I cleared a corner of the kitchen table and got busy. Really, really busy.

I took free business development courses. I wrote hundreds of letters, phoned the Government, went to local councils and begged important people to meet with me. With a posh voice I did my best to sound like I wasn't an unemployed girl in my spare bedroom – which I was. I researched funding sources and sent enough emails to break the internet.

Within one month of relentless activity, I had my first contract! I was to write and deliver local community programs, working with people to build confidence, train them to volunteer, address their health, wellbeing and more. Within six more months, we obtained a contract to train trainers across the Southwest of England to work with the disenfranchised. And I was still in my redundancy transition period!

I imagined my logo on the side of a great glass building, and determined that everything I was doing would honour all that the logo stood for.

During this whole process, I managed to create something quickly by simply remembering 'I love this', 'People need this' and 'Somehow I can do it'. Loving what you do is key to succeeding.

Now I talk a lot about cause and effect in my book about efficacy, 'The EFF Word'. It was here that my earliest experiences creating an 'efficacious existence' began.

⏸

Then suddenly, by a turn of fate, my redundancy was revoked, and I received a promotion! I know that if I hadn't faced this adversity (opportunity!), I wouldn't have started the business, and I would still have had 'just a job'. But incredibly, by wondering 'What can I do about this?' I now had a great job and a thriving business too!

I honestly believe I would not be where I am today if I had not embraced this adversity as an opportunity and an awesome blessing. Adversity always brings a benefit. It may not be easy. And it involves work. But by adopting the attitude that the very challenges which interrupt your journey are actually golden opportunities in disguise, if you say 'I am good enough to handle this,' your response can move you forward to create great things, and the interruptions can direct your true greatness.

To date, I have established this business in 3 countries, and our efforts are expanding every day.

Starting a business is hard. Everyone knows that. As entrepreneurs, many of us are self-taught. We learn to value the whole experience as we wade through our mistakes and exult in our victories. But having done it successfully three times, I've noted several distinct phases to succeeding in business.

In the next few pages, I would like to share 4 of my major philosophies and 4 key strategies to help you achieve similar success.

#1 *Normal* is the enemy, *Not Adversity*!

Each of us is on a path. Some paths are well-planned; others just 'happen'. Some of us get a job, go to work every day, and never vary from a daily routine which is totally unremarkable. We raise our family, keep the house tidy, and pay our bills on time. Day to day, nothing really changes. We think things like, "My job is ok, my relationships are ok, my finances are ok. Life is ok."

But this is *NOT OK*! This kind of 'normality' brings boredom, stagnation, and a dangerous life sentence of repetition! Your life is going nowhere, and international time zones can be set to your tea break! You deceive yourself with mantras like 'I'll keep working hard…,' or 'Maybe I'll win the lottery….' But can you really depend on the boss for a promotion? Or be sure that you're safe from redundancy? In the end, normal people are gripped with regret, admitting, 'I wish I had been brave enough to have tried…'

To be successful, you must break free from this death cycle of normality. Reject the mindset that adversity is something that 'happens to you'! Replace 'what if's' with a vision, and commit to trying something new! Yes, there will be great unknowns along the way. But consider the great artists and inventors. They embraced challenges as opportunities to create innovative solutions. It's time you left your comfort zone and pushed the boundaries of your potential! And the heroes we admire? They don't become heroes by doing normal stuff. They *choose their response* and actually *draw strength* from adversity! If you are to lead and succeed, you must consciously choose to **create** adversity, so that you can find the hero's way to trust it and transform it! It will only be as you stir the cauldron of chaos, skim off the dross of 'what doesn't work', and mold the molten metal of your gifts – only then will you become something great!

#2 Epiphanies are Lies

Are you waiting for an Epiphany, or some magical gift from the Universe to come save you? If so, you will have a long and futile wait. I hate to tell you, but the Epiphany isn't coming to change your life. No magical thought will mysteriously give you all the answers. That hope is worse than an illusion – it's a bold-faced lie!

Edison didn't *just invent* the light bulb.

Jobs didn't *just build* a MAC computer.

Every single great idea, every great business, every brilliant life is the result of years of vision, dedication, hard work, and progressive evolution. Your skills are a synthesis of all that you've done with your whole life.

Successful entrepreneurs don't get that way by just setting up a bank account, and BOOM! they are running a successful company. That does not happen.

So if you intend to start a business, you can't afford to sit there, waiting for 'your thing' to be revealed. The perfect idea, the perfect situation, the perfect solution? They don't exist! Do *something*. That is the ONLY way to find your niche. Every great creation has a point of conception, and then evolves. 'Nothing' cannot evolve; but 'Something', however tiny, can.

In 1878, Edison envisioned the light bulb. His team of inventors tried 999 things before getting it right. Follow his lead. Do something – anything! Then, like Edison, you will be progressively directed *as you take action*. You'll learn what works and what doesn't. From that first bold step, you'll gain new competencies and knowledge, enabling you to improve your plan – until you get it right!

#3 Be Willing to be the Butt of the Joke

I was ridiculed for wanting to do something audacious. So will you be.

Learn to be the BUTT of the joke. Without a sense of humour, I would probably be dead. Shit happens every day. It's tough. It's really, really hard.

Learn to look on the upside. Force yourself to see what you're learning when you're going against the grain. But most of all, Laugh!

Arthur Schopenhauer tells us that all Truths pass through 3 stages before being accepted. First, the new idea is ridiculed. People scoff that you can't do it. Second, it's violently opposed. They'll say, 'That can't be done.' or 'Why fix something that isn't broken?' Be ready for this opposition! Third, the new Truth is accepted as self-evident.

Now my mother is my biggest fan; she proudly announces to anyone who will listen that her daughter is a successful entrepreneur. She can't even remember those times when she doubted me. My success is just accepted as evident now.

Leaders, innovators, and entrepreneurs see the world differently than the rest of the population. We are visionary and futuristic. We see things that don't yet exist. This frustrates our friends, neighbours, and even our colleagues. They mock and oppose us, because they don't share our vision, and they resist change. Some are jealous, and some think, "Why didn't *I* think of that?" Perhaps they are afraid that they will lose us if we 'make it'. And some people are just assholes.

If you are determined to succeed, be ready for this oppositional mindset. You can't let it offend you. You see the world differently. You have a calling that they don't have, and a fire in your belly that will take you places they don't even dream of!

#4 Remember Who You Want To Be
A prominent theory of motivational behaviour identifies 4 distinct behaviours, which parallels my own theory about four kinds of people: *winners*, *normal people*, *losers* and *successful people*.

First there are the **Winners**. They are performers. They want to be *seen* to be the best.
Their psychological and physiological strokes come from winning, achieving, and being the best. These people are often very successful and win.

However, if one is to win, another has to lose. So this is not the greatest way of doing things.

Then there are the **Self-protectors**. Their psychological and physiological well-being come from not failing. As long as they personally don't fail, and the world doesn't end, everything is ok. I call these the *'normal'* people.

They are characteristically so frightened of adversity (because it can bring failure) that they never venture past *normal*. And this leads to a very unremarkable life.

Then there are **Helpless** people. They are convinced that they aren't good enough. They have given up. To them, everyone else can achieve, but they *'can't'*. This makes them the *'losers'*.

Finally, there is the *'Successful'* person. This person has mastery in his behaviour. He draws his well-being from simply being the best version of himself he can possibly be. He faces challenges as opportunities to grow and to learn. He is not in competition with anyone. All that is needed for him to succeed is to walk in the confidence that he is the best version of himself, and to constantly strive to become an even better version.

His progress is measured only from his own starting point. Nobody has to win or lose for him to be successful. Unlike the normal people, who follow a straight line in life, successful people take one fork in the road after another, always trying new things, learning, growing, and achieving.

Breaking into the Corporate Market

Building your business in the corporate market is all about gaining exposure, and building key relationships in the circles that count.

1. GAIN EXPOSURE and MEET YOUR CLIENTS

The first stage to succeeding in the corporate market is getting exposure. People need to know you exist. If you are like I was, nobody in the business world has heard of you before. When you're new, it's tough to get a foot in the door with the big boys. You need to find ways to get in front of your clients.

Identify where your target market can be found

Where do they do business? Network? Spend their down time? Which conferences do they attend?

Make a customer contact plan

Just as athletes make fitness plans, and writers make editorial plans, entrepreneurs make 'customer contact plans'.

2. ATTEND CONFERENCES, ROAD SHOWS, EXHIBITIONS
Make a list of conferences to attend

Categorize the conferences which your target market attends by theme and industry. Go to 'conference.com' or type in 'directory of conferences in (your city)' and make an excel sheet with the details: theme, location, dates etc. When I started out, I outsourced this list.

Get out there and GO!
Now get out to the conferences, road shows, and exhibitions like your life depends on it! Some conferences are pretty expensive, but the people who say they're a waste of money are doing it wrong. It's the best investment ever! You can share a two day event with someone, taking one day each. (But if you do this, it helps to be the same gender – thankfully nobody noticed that I was once called Robert!)

Network your Ass off!
Imagine how much time and money it would take to get a face to face meeting with 20+ of your decision making potential clients? In a conference, you meet them face to face! I once got the business cards of 300 target clients in a single conference. Within 12 months, I had been personally handed the cards of 2,000 of my direct clients – and spoken to them all! This is massive! I now have over 8,000 corporate contacts on my list.

Follow up immediately with the right email
The day after the conference, send a targeted email: 'It was great to speak with you at xxx conference." This tells them you are serious about following up with them. Add your photo in the email signature. (Remember - you're not the only person they spoke to.) But don't send some shitty email telling them all about your business and what you have to offer. This is your opportunity to offer help and add value – not the time for a sales pitch! Make it about *them*. Give them a free gift, or offer to meet for a free info-session about something they will love.

Host a booth
The next level of opportunity comes with hosting a booth. This is expensive, so when I was starting out I paired with organisations in a win-win situation. When you pair with another business, you can give your joint client an absolute beaut of a service. For instance, as a training business, I

approached other training organisations whose courses were different to mine, and we offered complementary collaborative services. They accepted every time, and we shared the cost. In addition, if they are established with a good reputation, you'll get a 'rub off effect'.

Outfit your booth
A well-prepared booth has all the marketing materials ready well ahead of the date. The conference pack will give you ideas. Make your booth attractive. Have at least one eye-catching and useful item with your logo and contact information: pens, USB car chargers, luggage tags, etc. If the item relates to your business, even better! Have all banners, fliers, business card holders, and bowls of mints ready. Collect contact information on an iPad, and stage a give-away as a lead-capture strategy!

3.   MILK YOUR TRAPPED AUDIENCE
Once at the conference, make the most of your trapped audience. They're trapped because they can't delete your email, or run off to a meeting. They can't pretend to be busy. They paid to come to the conference, which means they WANT to network. They are away from the usual stresses of the day, so you can get their undivided attention. And if they're manning a booth, they've got nowhere to hide! Capitalize on this! Get a colleague to man your booth, while YOU make the rounds, talking to every person about his business.

Take notes
Take notes on all they say, like 'We've been struggling with X'. That way, when you send out your emails the next day saying, 'Nice to meet you ...' you can add, 'Congrats on the X contract!' It makes a huge difference.

Grab those photo opp's!
Take a photo with them at their booth, and boom! you're immediately connected on LinkedIn, Facebook, etc. You're giving them exposure AND it's another chance for the 'rub off effect'.

Have fun and socialize!
They are normal people. Chat, laugh, have a joke, and for the love of God, stay and have a few drinks at the cocktail parties – THAT is where the real business happens, because that is when REAL relationships happen. Work time is over, people relax and become 'themselves' instead of their 'job title'. With a glass of wine in their hands they start asking about you, how you got where you are. You earn credibility and trust at the same time. I

once earned 6 figures worth of contracts while sitting around a gala dinner table – without knowing a single person before I sat down. Not bad for a fun night!

4. SPEAK AT CONFERENCES
This is the next level of exposure. This is your opportunity to be seen as THE go-to person in your industry, and where your conference list comes back into play. Standing on a stage at an industry conference automatically pedestals you as an expert. When they queue up to talk to me, no sales are needed! Getting a speaking gig also means the conference is free – DOUBLE bonus!

Decide which conferences matter
Getting that first speaking gig can be tough when you're a newbie. Ask the event organisers about the objectives and themes for the conference, and if they're looking for speakers. But don't just go 'Hey, can I speak at your event?' Identify their focus and determine how you can add value. Write a killer overview of the aims and outcomes of your speech. Read the LinkedIn profiles of the board members to see what they care about most. Contact them directly and ask, "What would be the best speech imaginable on your stage?" Again, make it all about them. If they reply, THEN share your speech plans, and follow up with a phone call. If they like your idea, they'll often influence the organisers to get you on stage. But stop short of being annoying. Even a whiff of desperation is a real turn-off.

Smaller events
For smaller events, contact industry groups, CCI, Rotary, clubs and businesses with an offer to deliver a free workshop or talk. An hour of your time can lead into big sales and great relationships. Always ask for a copy of the attendees list so you can email them all the next day. And always leave them with a call to action. Circulate a clipboard for contact information, offering a free consultation, membership on your Facebook page, or another relationship-building opportunity.

Final Tips
Get referrals
In addition to the four steps above, I arranged for others to promote my business for free. Yep!
I knew that if I boosted others' success while boosting my own, they would have an incentive to promote my services. For instance, when I first started in Australia, I helped large businesses secure funding to pay for their staff

training, which I then project-managed. First I connected with a tonne of training organisations and proposed a reciprocal arrangement: I would get a client funding and get them to use THEIR training services, and they would give me a cut of the fee they got from them as a finder's fee. In essence, I was getting them business for free. How could they refuse? This way I was paid by the client, made my commission from the training organisations, the training organisations were getting new business through me, and my client got his training funded, serviced and managed. Everyone was a winner. As a result, the training organisations referred me by telling their clients how their training could be funded, and the client then referred me to their business owner friends. You just can't beat this kind of business development!

When your success allows others to succeed and vice versa, your business will rocket launch!

Upsells
After I'd given them one great service, they were interested in other services – such as our training development. Once the relationships have been established, businesses prefer to stick with people who know and understand them. So when you sell service A, imagine how services X, Y, and Z could benefit them in the future, and start building relationships with the appropriate staff on their team.

Build relationships with key decision makers
As you build relationships with decision makers, there are a few keys to remember:

Let them talk
Find out about them, their pain points, their needs, and their greatest desires.
Speak their language
Know the industry terms, as well as the big contracts and projects going on in their industry, so that you can follow any small talk they bring up.
Be a human
Do not go into meetings with a straight face, a stiff suit and a PowerPoint presentation. Go in there with a personality, vibrancy, energy and an unwavering passion to give value to your client. Give your best advice, value, information and knowledge in the free consultation, so they will think, 'Crikey, if that's what I get for free, what must I get when I pay?'

Be flexible

My clients might be in a high-rise city block, or out in a remote, sweltering mine site. Ask the client where they would like to meet, and offer an open schedule. Some will suggest the office board rooms, a coffee, a lunch, or a dinner. I once met for beers in a remote mining town 'titty' bar!! The place they choose tells you what kind of person they are, how they like to do business, and it gives valuable clues as to what kind of approach to take with them. I have definitely done my biggest sales and made my longest, most profitable relationships over dinner and a bottle of wine. It pays to get them 'out of work mode' if you possibly can!

Final thought

I remember overhearing certain phrases when I was younger. One in particular which stood out for me was *'Life's a bitch'*.

My father's equivalent of this phrase every Monday morning was a defiant *'huuuuuff, back to reality'*. I remember thinking, *'Why is reality bad?'* One day as I watched him stuff his work boots on, puffing out this phrase, I asked, *"If you don't like your job, Daddy, then why do you do it?"*

My perspective is that life is not a bitch, life is *your* bitch.

At 17 years old, I was given the opportunity to learn a very, very powerful lesson. When a friend of mine was extremely sick with Chron's disease, I went to say my last goodbye. As I sat beside his bed, I was surprised to find him happy and optimistic – not what I expected to see from a dying man.

"Why are you so happy?" I asked him. He looked at me very seriously, saying, *"Sarah, I want you to remember one thing, and I want you to never, ever forget this."*

With his hand shaking hard, he picked up a glass of water and placed it on the table. *"Sarah, bad things will always happen to you. There are things in life you cannot control. Whether it's a mean, jealous person, a marriage break up, or a serious illness – stuff will happen, and this cup represents all of the bad things in life."*

Never forget that 100% of the time, you have a choice. When bad things happen, you can let them stop you. You can let them become the excuse and the barrier to everything you do. You can allow them to leave you stuck until, eventually, you die.

OR, when bad things happen, you can choose to see them as an opportunity. Ask yourself, 'What can I learn from this?' or 'How can good come from this?' With this as your mindset, you can walk victoriously to the other side of any adversity a better, wiser and stronger person than you were before it happened.

If my story can tell you anything, I hope it tells you this:
You are in control of everything in your life, *not* the adversities and challenges which you may be facing. You are in control of your life, your reality, your Monday morning, your job, your problems. Life is *your* bitch because you can choose how to respond to your challenges, and what you create as the result.

Anyone can choose to live like a mastery 'successful' person, and everyone has the ability to learn new skills to create a life of efficacious existence!

Sarah Cordiner

About the Author

Sarah is an author, qualified trainer, & global thought leader in 'Edupreneurship', 'Edu-marketing', Entrepreneurship, Efficacy and Education.

She is a specialist in training development and curriculum design, as well as trainer of trainers in adult learning.

She is the CEO of MainTraining; Winner of the 'Influential 100 Awards 2015'; Founder of 'The Edupreneur Awards', Founder of Edupreneur Magazine, Ambassador and peer advisor for 'TribeLearn' and The Institute For Professional Speakers and is a Nominee of The Telstra Business Women's Awards 2015.

Sarah's Keynote & Expert Topics:

- **Education**
- *Teaching & Learning Practices; The Hidden Curriculum; and Curriculum/Instructional Design and Development*
- **Entrepreneurship**
- **Edupreneurship**
- *What entrepreneurs and businesses in any industry can learn about growing business by using the platform of education instead of sales; and how to write profitable learning products and programs as a lead generation tool*
- **Workforce Planning & Development**
- *How corporates can maximise their productivity and profitability by effectively utilising their workforce skills and capabilities*
- **Students Transitioning From Education To Employment**
- *What's next and what do employers really want? What to do after your degree.*
- **Overcoming Adversity**
- *How actively creating adversity as well as effectively coping with it is the key to success in life and business*

Sarah's work has enabled the education of thousands of workers; helped welfare dependents in remote Australian communities (and throughout the UK) progress to employment, initiated the movement of 'Edupreneurship' and assisted other training providers to deliver excellent training.

"I have dedicated my life to providing engaging and transformative education to the world. I have designed, written and delivered curriculum to prisons, schools, universities, businesses, Government and charities internationally; as well as helped other training providers and entrepreneurs through edupreneurship, teacher-training and curriculum/instructional design".

With a PGCE, a BA (Hons) Degree in Education and 10 years in business, Sarah knows a thing or two about combining business with education to create a potent elixir of growth for entrepreneur and audience alike.

Follow Sarah: https://www.facebook.com/efficacyeffect

Treading My Own Path

Whatever course you decide upon, there is always someone to tell you that you are wrong. There are always difficulties arising which tempt you to believe that your critics are right. To map out a course of action and follow it to the end requires courage.
Ralph Waldo Emerson

As far back as I can remember I have been different from most people in that I've always followed my heart. When faced with making a decision, most people tend to stifle their intuition and rely on their mind, listening to their head rather than their heart.

Following your heart is not the easiest of things to do, in fact it is sometimes the riskiest and most challenging thing to do. But if you dare to be brave and listen to your intuition, your inner knowing and follow your heart, the rewards and happiness that it brings will be in abundance.

My name is Luke Sheedy. I founded and commenced an award-winning and successful holistic health practice in Brisbane over a decade ago. If I didn't follow my heart at the time, I would have never embarked on my entrepreneurial journey.

Commencing my business was taking the road less travelled. The quote by Robert Frost sums it up, "Two roads diverged in a wood and I – I took the one less travelled, and that has made all the difference."

I'm not going to lie, taking the entrepreneurial path and building a business from what was a random thought and idea, to eventually becoming a successful business in ten years has been a difficult, challenging and a bumpy path to travel. I have never stopped learning on this journey and I don't think I ever will.

I believe that you aren't born an entrepreneur, rather it's a fire that burns inside. It can be sparked by a dream, a fleeting thought, a goal, a talent or passion, or even a mentor or a circumstance.

For me, it was more like the spark of a flint before it became a fire inside, and my journey started when I was a young man.

After I left senior school, further educational studies were not an option for me. I grew up in a family environment that wasn't healthy for my soul. Like a lot of people, I was never encouraged or felt valued by my parents. This left me with very low self-esteem, no confidence or self-worth.

I quickly realised that I had to take responsibility and action for myself – my life was in my hands. In retrospect, growing up in a difficult family environment was the springboard I needed to be self-reliant. So I left the family home and stepped out into the big wide world as soon as I was able. I didn't think I was good enough, or could do anything of significance, I accepted mediocrity and took the first thing that came my way.

I started a traineeship in a local supermarket. I demonstrated a strong work ethic and had great interpersonal skills. I knew that I would make a great go of the job – which I did – working my way up the management ladder.

However, I soon realised that working in retail was hard, onerous work that didn't challenge me and didn't pay much more than minimum wage.

Working more than 12 hours a day on my feet, sometimes six days a week made the weeks long and tiring. I would do everything from stack shelves and help customers to ordering stock and managing a team and rosters. No matter how much overtime I did, no matter how much over target I generated in sales, no matter how much great customer service feedback I got, it was never enough. There was always more key performance indicators to meet and pay rises that never came.

Some days I would not even see daylight, starting at dawn and not leaving until after dark in the evening. It didn't take long for me to realise that this large supermarket chain wanted their pound of flesh and there were many other people lined up behind to take my job. I was easily replaceable and only as good as my payroll number.

This was the pivotal turning point for me, the spark that was slowly started to ignite. I thought to myself, "This can't be all there is to life?" Working so physically hard, with so much responsibility on my shoulders and a pay packet that just barely covers the bills with not much remaining. I really began questioning my life and my place in it.

I soon started to realise that people were living happy, abundant and fulfilled lives, I just wasn't one of them!

It was then that I started to accept that I didn't want to live an ordinary life. I wanted to live an extraordinary life.

After two long years, I resigned and decided that I wanted to work in a profession where I could help people, be of service and give value. I chose to get qualified and undertook studies in remedial therapies.

This is where a new world opened up to me and opportunities began to appear.

Soon after graduating, I decided that I was tired of working for large, profit-driven organisations and decided to start Human Energy. At the time, there were so many challenges I had to contend with.

Initially there was the financial risk as I had to use my life savings to fund it. This carried an enormous gamble, as working in retail it had taken me nearly ten years to save the nest-egg and I had nothing to fall back on. To jeopardise it all in a business that may or may not pay off was a daunting and overwhelming thought.

Additionally, as the business was a start-up, I had no clients on the books, no suppliers with established relationships and no presence in the market place.

From an emotional perspective, one of the biggest challenges was to overcome the fear and the self-doubt. Going from a guaranteed annual salary and most likely a job for life, with career opportunities to move up the middle-management ladder, all of a sudden I no longer had an income in my bank account each week. I feared that I had made a terrible mistake in giving everything up to follow my dream and pursue my passion.

I also had many friends, family and former colleagues giving me their (good-willed but negative) opinions about my new venture. I was given 'advice' that included excuses such as the time wasn't right, the economy wasn't strong enough, that I could never make a living, there were too many competitors, and the list goes on. This caused me to doubt myself, my skills and abilities to the point where it kept me from sleeping at night.

I learnt a valuable lesson in that negative people can bring you down and make you doubt yourself and your abilities. Don't listen to the naysayers and the dream stealers. Entrepreneurs believe in themselves and their dreams and when everyone says it won't work they say, "Just watch me."

I knew I had to stay strong and true to my vision of making this dream work, so I held fast and didn't give in to other people's negative chatter. I was stubborn, digging my heels in and knew from that day on, that this was my dream and it was up to me to make it work. I was creating my own reality.

Soon after starting Human Energy, there were weeks that went by when I only had a couple of clients and I was spending more money than I was making.

With persistence, hard work and determination, in time my client base started to grow organically. I would see one new client and through word of mouth they would refer their mum, sister, brother, friend, colleague. My reputation and client base grew exponentially in the first few years.

However, this growth was to be short-lived. The Global Financial Crisis hit and times became fiscally tight. Business confidence was down, unemployment rose and household budgets restricted. Holistic health treatments quickly became an unaffordable luxury in tough economic times. Local competitors also started undercutting each other on price to scramble for what clients they could.

I could have chosen to do the same and undercut on price or quality of service. But, that's not the entrepreneurial way. We are not guided by the dollar, we are authentic and want to be of service but are realistic in knowing that we need to pay our bills too.

My business suffered severely and my dream was diminishing. I had a decision to make, I could have blamed circumstance and easily given up. There were certainly doubts in my mind about how I could ever recover financially as my business was only a few years old and just getting established. However, now more than ever I was determined to hang in there, I had to see my dream come to fruition.

I truly believe that being committed, unwavering and following your heart is key to opening the doors to success and inner fulfillment. I have overcome many obstacles and challenges by listening to my intuition and believing in myself and my abilities, instead of following the herd or listening to others' opinions.

At this stage I could have allowed myself to feel powerless and taken the easy way out by closing the doors but instead I listened to my intuition and persevered.

I chose to tread my own path.

Some sage advice that I read from one of my mentors, Sir Richard Branson that resonated with me was, "You shouldn't be afraid to diversify if you are in a position to do so, especially because nothing ever stays exactly the same."

I heeded this advice and turned what was a negative into a positive. I adapted, and diversified my business to what the market was needing. Instead of focusing solely on remedial therapies, I evolved the business, focusing on counselling and coaching, taking a mind/body/spirit approach. This was the cornerstone of my success and a treasure in finding my true calling.

I overcame obstacles, instead of letting them overcome me. I chose not to be dis-empowered by circumstance. I focused on what I needed to do and became more flexible so I could adapt to change. I have outlasted competitors because I refuse to give in, never stop learning and above all, I am focused on making my dream work and therefore will do whatever it takes.

My philosophy on life is consistent with the simple saying, "If life gives you lemons, make lemonade." I strive to be the best I can be and I contribute my success to being flexible, through sheer hard work, determination and the ability to never, ever give up.

My business has evolved over the years and has continued to diversify. I also now focus my business on helping others to believe in themselves and harness their abilities and talents to achieve their goals and fulfil their dreams to live the life they want.

When I look back to when I first started, my mission statement was to help people to *"Live a Life Worth Living"*. It was my underlying purpose, in wanting to help people to live a great life. Now, even though the business has diversified, I still stand by that mission statement. I have had the resolve and purpose to stick with it and to learn all the steps along the way.

Now, I share my knowledge with others. Finding it difficult to keep up with demand for personal consultations, as well as having a work/life balance, I decided to write about my areas of expertise. My skills are multi-faceted thanks to my diversification strategy and include qualified counsellor, remedial and holistic health therapist, personal trainer, life advisor, motivator, entrepreneur and author.

I wanted to share what I had learnt throughout the years of working in my clinical practice. Many clients shared their inner conflicts, their lack of inner fulfilment, and feeling of being trapped in the status quo with no real meaning or purpose to their lives.

In my practice, I also treated many people young and old with depression. The black dog does not discriminate and with counselling and guidance many of my clients have been inspired, empowered and encouraged. With emotional blockages cleared, a positive mindset and reassurance, in time the dark clouds begin to clear and they can live the life they want and deserve.

My clinical practice enlightened me. And, it turns out that I'm not the only one who was never encouraged or felt valued as a young person growing up. So I took it upon myself to write a manual for living to address these concerns and provide the reader with the tools, strategies and direction so they can be encouraged to life a life worth living.

It is my determination and drive, combined with wanting to reach out to more people that prompted me to write *Discover Your Path, Your Life is Worth Living*. After having read many self-help books on my own path to self-improvement, I found that many books were difficult to read and complex, or just didn't make a connection with me, the reader.

Using this as an opportunity, I wrote with a style and tone that is conversational, as well as being informative and practical. It is an easy-to-read guide on how to reach inner fulfilment and follow your dreams.

It is a book that I wish someone had given me when I was a young man with no self-confidence, no direction and guidance. The self-help, motivational book is filled with the inspirational advice and guidance that I provide to my clients in one-on-one consultations.

The release of my book last year has been both a career highlight and a personal achievement. It is the culmination of many years of experience working with my Human Energy clients. Professionally it has opened up a whole new set of doors and opportunities, which I am grasping with both hands. As I have found out from my own experiences that when our visions open, our horizons expand.

I've overcome many challenges and obstacles to make my own dreams come true. This book is a journey of self-discovery (for myself and my readers). Many people told me I couldn't make my dreams come true. I wrote this book to encourage, to guide and to help people believe in themselves, just as I have done to get where I am today.

I have also been fortunate that I have had many 'small successes' along the way, such as winning accolades, which have cemented my reputation in the industry.

It is a great achievement to be able to live the life I once only dreamed of. I have a work/life balance that most people envy and I get to spend quality time with my baby daughter. I am not part of the rat-race and don't have to contend with office politics.

I am so passionate about helping people be the best version of themselves, it is an added bonus that I get paid well to do it. My greatest reward is not the financial remuneration, but helping clients be successful in their own lives. Hearing the many positive success stories of people achieving their dreams and knowing that I played a part in that is gratifyingly rewarding.

I have found that regardless of how illogical or irrational a decision may seem – if you follow your heart, and it feels right to you, you must take action. When you act upon it, you take responsibility for it.

Life is about taking risks and reaching out and soaring for your dreams. If you don't get opportunities, generate them. Create a niche, focus on the uniqueness of your product or service and stand out above the rest.

I have never stopped learning. I've always been of the belief that being an entrepreneur is a journey not a destination. By continually growing and persevering you will learn from your experiences and become a more confident you.

In summary, here are my top ten learnings:
- see the big picture, and then see bigger (but be realistic about your goals)
- never lose focus on your purpose
- make sure you have passion and perseverance
- be flexible, adaptable and diversify if you need to
- listen to your intuition and follow your heart
- continue to learn by reading relevant journals, papers and blogs and network with industry contacts to stay a step ahead
- remain authentic to yourself and your values and service
- you may fail at times, but accept it and learn and grow from your mistakes
- make a connection with your clients and customers, that is why they choose you over competitors
- be of service and give value and do it better than anybody else.

Don't live your life on auto-pilot, take the lead and put your hands on the wheel of your life and make the most of it, otherwise you allow others to control your destiny.

If you have a goal or dream that you want to fulfil, regardless of how large or small it is, it has to matter to you and only you.

When you sow the seeds of a better life for yourself, you will reap a great harvest of abundance in all aspects of your life. But to make it so, you have to put the effort and action in to create the results that you want. This choice is yours.

This life is worth living, we can say, since it is what we make it.
William James

The strength to follow your convictions

You can't connect the dots looking forward; you can only connect them looking backwards. So you have to trust that the dots will somehow connect in your future. You have to trust in something - your gut, destiny, life, karma, whatever. This approach has never let me down, and it has made all the difference in my life. - Steve Jobs

My life's story to some could seem scattered and a bit tumultuous; but there are a few ubiquitous themes: independence, entrepreneurship, diplomacy, and collaboration. Everything I've done, even selling peacock feathers as a child, has led up to my life's work: Hera Hub.

Before I dive into my history, I'll give you a flavor of my current business... Take a moment and picture a unique workspace inspired by the "spa": beautiful art, great lighting, lots of greenery, running water, fantastic smells, and soft, tranquil music playing in the background. Picture a place where hundreds of like-minded women support one another in business and beyond... creating a nurturing environment where each woman can find the resources she needs to be successful in every aspect of her life. Welcome to my world!

Throughout this chapter I will share the journey and path to launch Hera Hub, the challenges I faced, and what that's taught me as I continue to build an international business. I want to share my challenges, successes, and the wisdom I've gained over the last 40 years, but also get down the to the nitty-gritty, the nuts and bolts of business and how I was able to create something tangible, yet sincere (a word not often associated with business) by creating Hera Hub.

Enterprising Genes
I grew up in a small town on the Central Coast of California (Arroyo Grande). I was taught at a young age that money is not gifted but rather earned. While I envied my friends who received a weekly allowance, I'm now appreciative of my parents for teaching me this important lesson.

My first real business venture was utilizing a resource I had in my own back yard... peacock feathers. Growing up in a relatively rural area allowed us to have lots of pets, one of which was a pair of peacocks – Mr. & Mrs. Peabody.

At age eight I decided to gather up the beautiful male peacock feathers, which shed naturally each fall, and attempt to sell them at the corner grocery store for $1 each. The first day out I walked away with almost $80 in cash at age eight! This one event fuelled my entrepreneurial fire.

Parents

My parents got married young – both 21 – and dropped out of college (Fresno State) their third year. Neither of them ever completed their bachelor's degree. My parents moved from the San Joaquin Valley (thank God!) to the central coast to start a new life and business together.

My Father initially started a business in the every so glamorous field of addressing junk mail. During some weekend trips back to Fresno my Grandfather convinced him to take some rolls of carpet back to see if he could sell them. (After retiring from a career in banking my Grandfather opened a small retail floor covering business in Fresno.) With a drive to provide for his family, my Dad tried anything he could to make money in order to make ends meet. After many years of hard work he now has a thriving retail floor covering business that indeed provided for our family and more.

*One other side note: My Grandfather was a really unique guy. He was always engineering a pile of junk to create something interesting, like a self-driving 3-wheel bicycle. He was very patriotic, serving in World War II just after he and my Grandmother met. Later in life he purchased a vintage fire truck that he used to show off in all the local veteran's parades. You'll discover why this is ironic later in my story.

Dad – The Practical Business Man

I don't remember my Dad ever sitting down. Because his business was literally next door to our house he was constantly working. He was always on the move, building something new, making improvements here or there and fixing things around our property. He was always eager to teach me new things and encouraged me to get me involved in whatever he was doing. I don't think I remember him ever sitting on the couch and just relaxing!

Mom – The Artist

My Mom primarily supported my Father in the business, raised me, and also was very involved in her church and in the performing arts. My Mom still actively sings in the community choir and performs in Community Theater.

While my Mom didn't have a formal education or job description, she certainly wasn't spending any time on the couch either! In fact, she (for the most part) was responsible for building, not contracting out but actually building, the second story of our modest home and a barn at the back of our two-acre lot.

Family Name

I've always been proud of my unique first name. While it's often difficult for people to spell, it is memorable. How many people can say they own the domain of their first name? www.felena.com. I was named after my Great Grandmother, who was born in Sweden in 1900 and lived a full 88 years. I was lucky to get to spend the first part of my life with her.

Because I was an only child (which changed dramatically later) I had to be very imaginative. When I wasn't in school or doing chores I often came up with all kinds of games to play with myself and imaginary friends. That creative, unstructured play time allowed me to become comfortable by myself and very independent. I am also very social and enjoy the time I spend with family, friends and co-workers.

Divorce

I'm really not quite sure why my parents married to be honest. They were and are so different from one another. In the end it didn't work. They were married 8 years and divorced when I was 7. They fought openly and bitterly and I always remember thinking that I never wanted to be in that position. But that IS indeed the position I would be in just 22 years later.

Despite the battle, I was lucky... I had two parents that both loved me very much and continued to fight over custody until the day I was able (according to the courts) make my own decision. Not all Dads would fight so hard to spend time with their daughter.

New Beginnings

When my parents divorced my Mom decided to go back to school. She joined a specialized two year program in Animal Behavior at a school in Moorpark, California. Against my Father's wishes she moved me 3 hours south.

My Father was so dedicated to seeing me he would drive six hours round-trip every other Friday night to pick me up and bring me back to the central coast – his "every other weekend" rights. Then he would make the same trip on Sunday night to return me back in time for Monday morning class. He did this without fail for 2 years! He would sometimes drive down just to see me on random Saturdays if he wasn't able to spend the entire weekend with me.

My Life in a Zoo

My Mom moved back to the Central Coast just before my 9th birthday. Due to her specialized training, she landed a job as the manager of the Atascadero Zoo. Every day after school (5th & 6th grade) I would walk to the zoo and spend the afternoon with my Mom there. It was like living in a dream! I helped out with small chores and got to see the most amazing things!

No one would believe me now, so thank god I have pictures, but we actually had an opportunity to take care of two baby tigers in our home for about a month. The mother tiger rejected her two cubs at birth (probably because she was pissed that she was in captivity) so my Mom, as the manager, had to take them home and bottle feed them. You can imagine the conversation in school, "So do you have dogs/cats/fish?" "Yes, and I also have two baby tigers!"

Shortly after moving to Atascadero, my Mom met my now step-Father, Steve, and got married. Ironically my Dad followed suite shortly thereafter. I was blessed, as both my step-parents (Steve & Susan) were and are wonderful people. And I believe perfect for my parents. I vividly remember feeling happy for each of my parents when they found their true love. They both remain married to their second spouses today.

The More the Merrier!

Although I grew up as an only child for the first 9 years of my life, that all was about to change! Susan, my new step-Mom, had two sons around my age. Peter was just three weeks older than me and Matt was two years younger. It was a bit awkward having to learn a new way of living and sharing but we got through it.

Not long after getting remarried, both my parents decide to have a second child. My Dad and Susan had John, my half-brother, when I was just 11 and my Mom and Steve had Hannah just one year later. In a silly way, it seemed as if they were in competition with each other!

Steve wanted more children and my Mom had always wanted to adopt (something she and my Father fought bitterly over). So shortly after having Hannah, my Mom brought home a sibling group of 3 foster children, which she later adopted. She then adopted one other child from a woman in her church whose daughter was not able to raise "Selma", as my Mom named her.

During this time my Father and step-mom had also had a child, John Hanson – named after my Grandfather. I was complete with a family of 8 brothers and sisters!

So, in a short few years I went from being an only child to having eight brother and sisters!

Lessons Learned
I feel like everything I learned as a child and young adult had led me to the point where I am now and I owe a lot to both of my parents.

Lessons learned from my Mom – My Mom taught me to follow my intuition and to see beauty in everything. She showed me the importance of self-expression is important and proved that you could be elegant even in overalls.

Lessons learned from my Dad – My Dad taught me the importance of hard work, determination and confidence. He showed me that building anything from businesses to relationships, requires patience and follow-through.

By showing me that they loved me unconditionally, my parents instilled me with a strong sense of self and by making me work for everything I received, I became confident in my abilities rather than developing sense of entitlement. This combination has given me a true sense of self-worth which has gotten me through some extremely difficult times.

College Bound?
Through working in my Father's business I found that I had a knack for sales and creativity. The logic of business just clicked with me from an early age. While I was involved in my high school's business club, DECA, I wasn't a dedicated student. In fact I got mostly C's. Apparently I was far too

interested in boys than class! One of those boys was Ryan Ripley, a handsome boy 4 years older than me. He worked for the local fire department and lived just down the street. We dated my junior and senior year. We broke up right after High School, as I felt I needed to experience other relationships. I just seemed to have something for fire trucks...

Since my parents never received their bachelor's degrees there wasn't a strong push for me to go to college. My Dad hated school; he found it impractical and a waste of time, so he gave me a choice. He made it clear that he would pay for college or I could take the same pot of money and use it to start my own business or put a down payment on a home. Since I realized I wasn't wise enough to invest in a home or start my own business, I decided I'd better continue my education.

Since my GPA wasn't adequate to get into a decent college, I decided to go to the local community college for two years with the goal of transferring to a four-year school. I thrived in the new environment and I was able to get my grades up and focus in on the subjects I enjoyed. With a better GPA I was accepted to private school – University of San Diego – and ended up graduating with honors.

Exploring the World
One of my weakest subjects was foreign language. I couldn't pass Spanish to save my life! Somehow I got around it in High School, but the college requirement was looming. I somehow convinced my Dad to allow me to do my language requirement in Spain, through a study abroad program (I promised to pay him back, which I did). I immersed myself in Spanish culture for two months and then travelled around Western Europe for a month after. I was lucky enough to meet a travel companion while taking classes in Spain since I didn't know a single person when I arrived. Shawna and I travelled through Spain, Italy, Switzerland, and France together for three weeks. She had to return home and I was on my own, in Europe, for one final week. I have to say that week was one of my defining Moments. I was 20 years old, sleeping on trains, exploring cities alone and no one in the world knew where I was. It was liberating!

Run Felena, Run!
Along the way I gained a passion for running. It's funny, because while I played tennis all four years of High School, I had always hated running! I guess it came out of necessity, as I wasn't playing sports in college and needed a way to stay in shape. I enjoyed it so much that ended up running

two marathons in college. I wasn't the fastest runner and averaged a 10 minute miles in training, but I finished each marathon in just 3 hours and 45 minutes! I guess it was adrenaline and my competitive spirit coming out!

Close-to-Death Experience

Although I wanted to get into Marketing, I took a job right out of school in Sales. It was a simple decision, working in sales meant I was earning more money and had more opportunities. I moved to Los Angeles and took an inside sales position for a large dental company. Less, than a year later I moved to another sales job in the equally exciting industry of commercial office furniture!

I was in that position for just a few months when I took a weekend trip back to San Diego to visit some friends. Nothing could prepare me for what was about to happen.

It was May 6th, 1996 at about 9pm - I was exiting the freeway in Ocean Beach (via a bit of a blind intersection). A fire truck ran the red light at about 40 miles per hour and collided with my small Jetta. No air bag, no lap belt, nothing. At 22 years old I came literally inches away from losing my life. It took the emergency crew well over an hour to pull the fire truck off my car with a crane and then use the Jaws of Life to pry me out. I was conscious, but in shock, the entire time. I broke well over 20 bones in my arms, legs, and face... including my clavicle and pelvic bone. The doctors told my Father I would likely never run again.

It was a long road to recovery; I went through dozens of surgeries, some immediately, some in the following years. I still have residual challenges, as I have enough titanium in my body to build a small robot. I was in the hospital over a month and confined to a wheel chair for several months following. I moved back to Arroyo Grande to live with my family. My sweet boyfriend from San Diego took a leave from UCLA Art School to help take me to all my physical therapy appointments that summer.

Lesson Learned

There are so many things one learns from an experience like this. The accident gave me, my family, and everyone around me an incredible perspective on life. I believed that because I survived it, I must have been put on this earth to do something important.

I also learned very early on that none of us know when our last day on this earth might be and we must live each day as if it was our last!

Your time is limited, so don't waste it living someone else's life. Don't be trapped by dogma - which is living with the results of other people's thinking. Don't let the noise of others' opinions drown out your own inner voice. And most important, have the courage to follow your heart and intuition.   Steve Jobs

Back to Los Angeles
It was a full six months until I returned to Los Angeles and was able to get back to work with the furniture company. Within a short period of time I was promoted to outside sales, which I enjoyed tremendously. That job was really my first taste of collaboration and relationship building.

About a year later I had my first opportunity to move into marketing with a high tech recruiting firm in Torrance. I was elated! My first marketing job!

Meanwhile on the personal side I married my boyfriend of 3 years, Brian, who had faithfully stayed by my side during my recovery process. It was remarkable for a twenty-one year-old man to have the wherewithal to stay with me through my recovery. I can tell you I wasn't pretty – I pretty much looked like a squashed blueberry for a while.

Even though my friends vividly remember me saying "I don't think I want to settle down" and that International Business was my main goal, I felt indebted to Brian and obligated to say yes when he asked me to marry him a little over a year after I recovered. I remember thinking that we were young but I couldn't see not marring him after he stood by me through thick and thin! We married in September 1998.

First Layoff
I was shocked to find out that only 9 months after landing my first real job in marketing that the company was sold and the majority of the staff was

going to be laid off. I was devastated. I was recently married and now supporting my artistic husband in his ventures to launch a surf board manufacturing and apparel company. I needed to find a new gig quickly.

After repainting every inch of our house (remember Hansons don't sit still) I landed a job at a full-service marketing agency in Redondo Beach in less than two months. We did work for clients such as DIRECTV Sports, Sun America, Fox News Channel, and Epson. My job grew into a role where I helped manage collaboration projects between companies like DIRECTV Sports and large retail merchandisers.

As if I wasn't busy enough, I decided to go back to school a few nights a week to get my MBA. Unfortunately the marketing agency was having problems (two partners who fought relentlessly) and I was laid off again in 2000. I took the opportunity to finish my MBA by cramming 22 units in one semester before moving back to San Diego in 2001. I was OVER Los Angeles!

Fresh Start
Because of the recent burst of the tech bubble, my job prospects were bleak. We ended up settling in an artistic area of San Diego (North Park) and I eventually found a job as Director of Marketing (after a short stint working for the Mexican Mafia -- I'll save that for another story) with a high tech company where again my role was to manage collaborative projects with large media companies such as CNN, USA Today, and LA Times. I definitely felt like I was in over my head at the time but I somehow had the confidence to take the "fake it till you make it" attitude. An attitude I have routinely applied throughout my career. My other mantra is "say yes and Google it"!

The founding team ended up selling the company to America Online in 2003, which meant I was again out of a job... my 3rd layoff by age 29!

I had a couple options at this point. I could find another J-O-B (which to me seemed like a death-sentence) or create my own business. I'd been the family bread winner for five years and felt it was my turn to follow in my Father's footsteps! Plus, San Diego as a city is extremely supportive of small businesses and I felt that the possibility of success was just as high creating my own company as it would be going to work for another company that would be bought, sold, downsized, etc.

Entrepreneurship

With a solid background in marketing I launched my consulting practice in 2003. I named my business Perspective Marketing, as I felt I could help small businesses see issues from an objective angle. Over the eight year period my niche emerged in helping small service based companies grow through relationship marketing. Of course I took a huge pay cut - it took me several years to even get to close to the salary I was earning in high-tech - but it was worth it. I had freedom and control of my destiny!

Part of the reason I got my MBA was because I eventually wanted to teach. I had imagined it was something I would do after I retired at 55 but when I took the opportunity to branch out on my own I thought I might try my hand at teaching sooner than later. Through a series of connections, Cal State University Dominquez Hills and Cal State University Long Beach offered me an adjunct teaching position in marketing for their online programs. Shortly after that I also landed a job teaching Entrepreneurship at the Fashion Institute of Design & Merchandising (FIDM), downtown San Diego. This gave me some stable income while I launched my business and I also found I LOVED it! I especially enjoyed teaching young women at FIDM!

I WILL Run Again

My Dad had gotten into running around the same time I did and later decided to run his first marathon. I thought this might be a good opportunity for me to see if I could complete another marathon. It had been almost 10 years since my car accident... I figured I would be OK. I'm proud to say both my Father and I completed the Rock-n-Roll marathon! My time was nowhere near my college days but at least I could say I did it! See I proved those doctors wrong! It was however my last marathon. I am now satisfied with running half marathons!

At age 31, six years after marrying my college sweetheart, my husband and I split up. Simply put, we married too young and his eyes wandered... twice.

Lessons Learned

Surviving the accident and the end of my marriage taught me that I could recover from anything and that what doesn't kill you can truly make you stronger. Through each change, I learned that reinvention is an important part of life and being willing to redefine my personal goals and professional life was absolutely necessary for not only my survival but my success.

Starting my own business after the job losses helped me believe that I could control my own destiny.

Growing My Network

Shortly after I launched my business I realized I must start focusing on building connections and strategic alliances. Through this, I really learned how to "network".

In 2006 I met at talented attorney from Texas, Linda Lattimore, as she was in the first stages of launching a professional organization, Women's Global Network. WGN's mission was to build local business connections and help women in developing nations launch small businesses through microloans.

I was one of her first board members and just over a year later took over the leadership of the San Diego chapter, as she moved back to Texas for a job and to launch additional chapters. Running WGN not only gave me great leadership experience but also good visibility. I continued to expand my network and meet amazing business women throughout San Diego.

My eight-year affiliation with the Fashion Institute led me to launch a fashion networking organization and do several non-profit projects, including a venture with the San Diego Visual Arts Network called "Art Meets Fashion". This was a unique collaboration project pairing visual artists and fashion designers throughout San Diego. In addition to the artist/designer duo, each team was also comprised of a documenter (photographer or videographer) and educator. The goal was to document the creative process between artist and designer and for the educator to take the learnings back into San Diego high schools and community colleges to inspire teens to get into the arts. The work was showcased at the San Diego Airport from March to September 2011 and at various galleries and boutiques in Central San Diego.

This continued to build my drive to collaborate!

Kids

A common question is "do you have children"? My smart-ass answer when I taught college was "yes, I have 30"... referencing my students at FIDM who were mostly young women between 17-20 years-old. It's a fair question but one I've struggled a bit with. My "clock" has never ticked. While I like kids, I never felt the urge to have my own. This is despite my

Father telling me on a daily basis that having children was the best decision of his life.

But this is a tough choice for a lot of driven women. Do you step off the success wheel to have a child? How will this change your life? Each woman needs to make her own decision but for me, the way I like to put it is, "I'm better to give my attention to many people vs. one or two".

Incubating New Business Ideas
After leading WGN for two years, I had the opportunity to step into a temporary leadership position with Ladies Who Launch. I took over management of the local chapter in August 2009. This was an opportunity to work with a new group of entrepreneurial women and with a national organization that had fairly good brand recognition. I've really enjoyed leading the Incubator Intensive Workshops – which are part inspiration, education, and accountability between 6-8 female entrepreneurs.

I took the concept of collaboration to the next level when I joined forces with Michelle Bergquist, founder of Connected Women of Influence, to launch the Business Women's Mega Mixer in 2010. This is a showcase of professional women's organizations throughout San Diego County. The first event drew over 25 organizations, 500 women, and raised thousands of dollars for a local female-focused non-profit.

Lesson Learned
While I had leaned a tremendous amount through teaching, networking and building my business, I was starting to get burned out and with as social as I was, working at home was hard for me. And I was starting to get burned out wearing multiple hats. At one point I had 5 business cards and over a dozen email addresses!

As Michael Gerber describes in the "E-Myth" (Entrepreneurial Myth):
Everyone that starts a business is a technician that suffers from an Entrepreneurship seizure. Small businesses do not work the way intended because the technician only works in the business and cannot also have the foresight to work on the business at the same time.

I was pretty burned out and needed to create a business that was bigger than myself, something I could scale!

Where it all came together

Hera Hub really grew out of my need. I worked from home for eight years, and while it's great for the convenience, and is of course cost effective as a small service based business, it has its downfalls. It can be distracting and isolating working from home. The laundry and dishes nag at me, the dog whines, the doorbell rings, anything can take my attention away from what I NEED to be doing! Privacy and the desire to appear professional were also major concerns when I was working from home.

This day-time challenge was coupled with the struggle to find evening event space for my networking groups. Hotels and private rooms were always too expensive and community centers were closing left and right.

I was turned on to the concept of coworking in 2008, when I hosted a networking event at San Diego's first coworking space, the Hive Haus. I pondered the idea of opening my own space for a couple years before really diving in to do market research. I ended up visiting coworking spaces in New York, Los Angeles, and San Francisco in June of 2010 and started to look for spaces in late summer.

Challenges in Commercial Real Estate

The commercial real estate process was much more complex and challenging than I ever imagined. I had two strikes against me: a new business and a new concept - no one wanted to take a risk. I got patted on the head more than a few times from older men in this very traditional industry.

I spent 3 months negotiating my first deal directly with a building owner who was interested in the coworking model (without a broker). That blew up in the 11th hour when he decided to launch his own coworking space - after I'd shared my extensive business plan and all my financials. History repeated itself (although this time I was armed with a broker) when negotiating my second deal. We got all the way to the day I was to get a cashier's check for the deposit and first month's rent only just to have the building owner tell me, they found a better fit for the space.

I was devastated. I remember thinking that maybe it wasn't meant to be after all.

My third lease negotiation also got off to a rocky start. After submitting my proposal I found out the building was in escrow. After waiting three weeks for the new owner to respond, we finally got a chance to meet. Much to my delight the new owners knew about coworking and had visited the Hive Haus. They seemed to be interested.

We began the negotiation process on the ideal space, about 3,700 square feet, when they got a bid from a tenant in an adjacent suite who wanted the space. I thought I was doomed! The building owners came back with a suggestion to look at a suite in the adjacent building. The space was over 8,000 square feet, which they agreed could be split. With a little vision I sectioned off close to 5,000 square feet and put in a new proposal. It was a big risk, as it was almost twice the size of the prior two spaces.

Now, mind you... I had no clue about commercial construction and what was feasible. Luckily I didn't have to hire an expert because my long-time partner, Keith, is a contractor. He was able to advise me throughout the process, his expertise was a God-sent!

Ready, Fire, Aim
I had recently read a book by author Michael Masterson, which gave me the drive to try a different tactic. It was early April 2011 when I met Amy Mewborn, the recent franchisee for Xtend Barre (a popular form of Ballet-meets-Pilates). She overheard me lamenting about the commercial real estate industry at a networking event. She mentioned her newly launched location, not far from where I was looking, and invited me to take a look at a second dance studio she wasn't yet using.
I went the next day to look at the 700 square foot studio (which happened to boast dark brown hardwood floors and aqua walls – pretty much Hera Hub colors) and wrote her a check on the spot for a temporary lease. Keith amazingly rigged a ledge on one of the ballet bars, so we could run power and helped me buy and set up IKEA furniture in just one week! We even set up a make-shift meeting room in a storage space. We made it work!
I officially opened the "temporary" Hera Hub on tax day, April 15th 2011. Despite the mirrored walls and the intermittent sounds of women groaning through leg-lifts, I was able to create what I now call "spa-inspired"... complete with candles, fountains, and soft music. I opened our doors for four months to anyone who wanted to try out the shared workspace for free. I could start to see it come together!

Control
It's not a pretty word, yet it's the word I use. Another lesson gifted to me was that of the 2008 stock-market crash. My stock portfolio (like everyone

else's) took about a 40% blow. While launching Hera Hub was a risk, I invested close to $60,000 of my own money and borrowed an additional $30,000 from my Father, I felt like I was at least "in control" of the outcome. I felt I had NO control leaving the money in mutual funds with companies I didn't even keep track of. Succeed or fail, at least I knew I was in control of my money!

Final Stretch

I continued the negotiation process while running the temporary space. I was elated when we finally came to an agreement. Despite the road blocks, my dream was becoming a reality!

We finished construction in early August and I officially opened the doors of the first Hera Hub on Monday, August 15, 2011. A full year after I started to look for space.

I truly feel everything I've done in my life led me up to the moment of launching Hera Hub. It is a natural extension of the collaboration I have fostered throughout my entire career. It has taken a lot of 80 hour work weeks, but I'm proud to say Hera Hub is a huge success! We grew to over 150 members in the first year and launched our second and third locations in San Diego County to respond to the demand. We now have three successful locations and are expanding globally through a franchise model.

My next goal (our vision) is to help over 20,000 women launch and grow their business through 200 locations globally over the next five years!

What is Hera Hub?

Hera Hub is a shared, flexible work and meeting space where entrepreneurial women can create and collaborate in a professional, productive, spa-like environment. The platform provides our members with connections to other business experts, access to educational workshops, and visibility within the community... thus giving them the support they need to be prosperous.

Beautiful, yet Functional, Coworking Space

Unlike other coworking spaces that tend to focus on recreating typical office settings, all of the Hera Hub locations were designed to benefit all five senses. Our coworking spaces focus on the five senses:

1. Sight – beautiful art, live plants, calming colors, friendly faces
2. Smell – aromatic candles that relax and invigorate

3. Sound – soft spa-like music and tranquil running water
4. Feel – variety of comfortable seating arrangements, including standing work stations
5. Taste – fresh brewed coffee, tea, spa water and snacks

Who Was Hera?

Significant thought process went into developing the name and logo. Hera, the Greek Goddess of women, was revered as being the only Goddess who accompanied a woman through every step of her life; blessing and protecting her family and financial security. Hera represents the fullness of life and affirms that women can use their wisdom in the pursuit of any goal they choose. How is it that the beautiful peacock was her symbol? Perhaps I already knew what my quest in life was when I was selling feathers at the grocery store.

Why Women?

I truly believe that women interact differently and are instinctively more collaborative in their approach to business. I felt it was important to create a space for female entrepreneurs that is not only beautiful, comfortable, and feminine but also very professional.

Many women running small businesses also have to juggle family life, and therefore feel an affinity with other women in the same situation. A supportive environment where women feel they easily relate to others helps get to that point in the relationship where they know, like, and trust the other person and are `therefore more likely to ask for feedback or refer business.

Hera Hub Myths

- *These women are just building hobby businesses*. Our members are providing for their families and making a much larger economic impact. In fact, as of 2013 there are over 8.6 million women-owned businesses in the United States. Those are not hobbies!
- *There must be cattiness - how could 300 women get along so well?* When you encourage women to support each other and collaborate, there simply isn't the time or space for fighting or backbiting.
- *Or my favorite… "oh you must have pillow fights and girl talk all the time"*. While we certainly enjoy each other's company, we are here to work. And we work HARD!

Recap: Lessons Learned

Looking back over the 40 years of my life, I can safely say that everything I experienced, the good and the bad, lead me to where I am today and will continue to propel me forward.

The Lessons Learned in Childhood

My childhood taught me to recognize and utilize the resources available to me, to work hard and try my best. From my Father I learned to be persistent, resilient and creative. My mother instilled the importance of presentation and trusting my gut.

The Lessons Learned in my Early Career

Although I didn't intend to start my career in sales, my childhood had taught me to jump on the opportunities as they presented themselves. My accident taught me to value my health and family and to live life to the fullest. Knowing that things can change in the blink of an eye makes me more mindful of using every day.

The Lessons Learned in my First business

Making the jump from being employed to being self-employed was unsettling but I knew pursuing my dream wasn't any more dangerous than relying on someone else's ability to provide me with a steady job. I also learned that in order to be my best, I couldn't say "yes" to every opportunity that presented itself. I needed to be deliberate in the choices I made and avoid becoming distracted by projects, objects or commitments that pulled me away from my long term goals.

The Lessons Learned at Hera Hub

Women are amazing business owners - we can take an idea and build a successful business model even if we are repeatedly told "no" and have to start in a small room with a wall full of mirrors.

Final Challenge

I have built this business--literally. Installing curtains, assembling furniture, putting in the final nail — I believe the extreme attention to detail (aesthetics and atmosphere) makes the space. I would stay up hours, making sure every inspirational wall-decal was placed in just the "right" spot.

One biggest challenge in franchising will be to ensure that I select the "right" women to build the Hera Hub platform internationally. I need to find women who have the same passion and attention to detail... women who want to build a strong community and support other women. Wish me luck!

Final Advice

Go Big or Go Home!
I encourage you to challenge yourself – set goals, work hard and show up for your business. There is no one there to tell you how to manage your time, when to say "yes" to certain tasks and when to say "no", so you need to trust your gut and your abilities and when you are unsure, ask for help. Admitting uncertainty to a group of trusted advisors allows your colleagues to do the same and allows them to help you. Don't be afraid to ask, the worst thing you hear is a "no" and I can guarantee that you will hear a lot of those as you grow your business.

Moving Forward
No matter what stage of your life or business you are in, being honest, sincere and reliable is an absolute necessity. Find something you love and do it well. Our lives are too short to spend them staying stagnant. I encourage you to keep growing - as I continue growing the Hera Hub brand and growing personally, I know there is more to learn and that this is just the beginning of something truly beautiful.

Felena Hanson

Picking up the Pieces

Up until 1997 I'd had a great life with some wonderful experiences. I had been to university and completed a science degree and later a Master of Marketing, married my childhood sweet heart and celebrated 20 years together in August 1997, lived in England for 3 years and travelled the world for 1 year. When we came home to Australia, we bought the house of my dreams in a fabulous old suburb and renovated it into the exact the house I wanted. In March 1997 I got promoted to the best job I had ever had as a national business unit manager for one of the world's largest software companies – a business unit that was created as a result of my marketing plan. I cancelled our planned holiday in Europe and worked hard to recruit 10 people to bring a complete business unit together from scratch in just three months.

Sounds good huh? Well on the surface it was. I had almost all I wanted, with the exception of a child that I had wanted all my life but not been able to have. Then it all seemed to just fall apart.

In September, my boss restructured me out of my own business unit and made me redundant. I was devastated. That group was my baby and I didn't even get a chance to show what I could do with it. Just before Christmas my husband confessed he was having an affair. I must admit, I did know, but I didn't want to know. It was a work affair and they all knew at his work before I knew. He hadn't been subtle about it. I felt professionally as well as personally embarrassed as the organisation he worked for had been my largest client in the job I had just lost. It felt like a bigger betrayal for that reason.

So I ran away to England to visit friends. I had sacrificed my April holiday to Europe for my new role, so after losing my job, I kept pushing my husband to book another trip to Europe with me. He kept deflecting it saying he had too much work on. Well, I found out what he had actually been working on, didn't I?

I booked my flight to London on Christmas Eve and left on New Year's Day. I love skiing so I also booked a 2 week skiing trip to Val Thorens, France, on my own in a chalet full of strangers. It was a lot of fun and I was enjoying being on the snow again, shushing down the fabulous slopes and putting on a brave face to have some fun. Then, at the beginning of the second week, after seeing someone else get hurt on the slopes, I had a thought, "If I was hurt, then my husband would have to stay and look after me and not leave me."

Well, that was a great lesson for me in creating what I think about. The very next day I fell on the first run of the day and completely obliterated my anterior cruciate ligament in my right knee as well as tearing more than half my medial ligament and damaging other ligaments in my knee and hip. It was a good one. I don't do anything by halves. In retrospect, I wouldn't recommend anyone go skiing or do anything so physically risky when in such an emotionally vulnerable state. It's not a good idea.

So I returned to London and then home to Melbourne a week later on the Tuesday. Saw the surgeon on Thursday, booked my operation for the following Thursday. My husband moved out of our house on the Sunday. He had said he would stay and look after me but he couldn't stop seeing that woman. Mum gave me sound advice in saying that would be too much for me to cope with, so I asked him to leave immediately instead. It was an incredibly heart breaking, tear filled time. He also shed a few tears, so it was painful for him too. It was a sad way to end a 20 year relationship, especially one I didn't want to end.

I had my knee re-construction operation on 12th of February. It was my 38th birthday on the 15th and our 11th wedding anniversary on the 28th. Not very happy celebrations at all. A couple of weeks after my operation it looked like my wound might be infected. I remember my physiotherapist asking if I was sleeping badly or feeling depressed; signs of an infection. I told her yes but that was to be expected considering my husband left me 4 days before the operation. Her response was "The bastard!"

It turned out my leg was infected, so I went in for my second operation of half day surgery to have that drained. It was more serious than expected and the infection was on the staples into my bone so my half day stay in hospital turned into 3 days on an antibiotic drip. I felt so depressed, especially being in a ward with all old ladies having their hips done. The infection wouldn't go away despite many antibiotics, so 10 weeks after my first operation, I had a third one to remove the staples and the screw and do a full arthroscopic cleanout of as much scar tissue as possible. That did the trick.

Add to all of this, my house was burgled when I made an emergency dash to my psychologist after being told I had to have a third operation. The intruder smashed a window and cut themselves on the way in and then left blood on everything they touched in my house. It was very traumatic when already in a highly distraught state, to come home and see the bloody t-shirt hanging out of my lounge room window and blood throughout my house. Then I had to deal with police and insurance and trying to work out what had been stolen as well. As if I didn't have enough to cope with already.

All of this occurred in just over 6 months of my life in 1997-1998.

This whole process meant that I was on crutches several times and for the major part of the 14 weeks post skiing accident, rather than commencing rehabilitation. There I was trying to learn to live by myself for the first time in 13 years, and being a cripple who couldn't walk or drive most of the time. It is not easy to carry shopping and manage crutches at the same time. Most of the time I found myself walking around the supermarket leaning on the shopping trolley for support and crying. I must have looked a real treat.

I just couldn't stop crying. It felt like there was a big gaping hole in my stomach where I used to live with my great job and not unhappy relationship. I started keeping a journal when I got home from hospital after my second operation. In it I stated that I was not unhappy in the relationship, but was not happy or fulfilled either. I used to think I was about 70% happy and something was missing but I didn't know what. Now I can look back and see it was "me" who was missing from my life and I was lucky if I was 50% happy.

So 1998 was a very difficult year filled with the most intense physical and emotional pain I could imagine, or could not imagine until I experienced it. Trying to get my leg to go straight again was an agonising struggle. I ended up having to wear a brace from thigh to ankle for 6 weeks that pressured my knee to go straight. By the time I could actually stand on my own two feet I had to learn to walk again because my muscles had atrophied to thin little strips down my leg. It was not a good look with a really skinny calf and thigh and a big fat knee in the middle. I looked like something out of a cartoon. It is a very weird feeling having to consciously instruct my leg and foot to bend and move properly to do something that has been totally unconscious almost my whole life.

That big black hole remained in my stomach and my tears kept flowing for many months. At one stage I wrote "I wish my tears were like rain so at least I know they will stop one day". My family doctor kept telling my parents I must be depressed and would need anti-depressants because I could not go through all that without getting depressed. After crying my way home for an hour at Easter, while I was driving, I acknowledged I couldn't cope and maybe I did need the medication.

The thing is, I didn't just sit there in my black hole of despair and feel sorry for myself. Don't get me wrong, I felt plenty sorry for myself at times. I was not only grieving the loss of my best friend and partner in life with whom I had shared so much, but also for the loss of the future I had planned with him; having children, spending time with friends, growing old together and all the things I had thought we would do together. As well as that I was mourning the loss of the highest level job I ever had and dealing with being out of work. I often felt like I had nothing to live for, but that didn't mean I did not want to live.

In many ways my life had fallen apart and I had lost all that I measured myself by; my job, my relationship and my body (my physical health and fitness had always been important to me). They had all failed on me and had rejected me. I felt not wanted by anyone. In my journal I said "Surely somebody wants me. I'm good enough to be wanted by someone for something." I couldn't get a job and was on my own at home most of the time. It was a very tough phase to go through and a real beating to my confidence and self-esteem.

I was determined that I was not going through all of this pain for no reason. I was going to come out of it a better person on the other side and rise like a phoenix from what felt like the ashes of my life. I took steps to help me process my grief, help me deal with my life changes and help me integrate what was happening so I could define what I needed to keep going and rebuild my life.

I saw a clairvoyant and she gave me the best advice I could've got at the time. She said "Stop focusing on what you have lost and focus on what you do have." When I thought about it, I did still have a lot. I still had my beautiful house, which I loved living in and could have some great parties in. I didn't have the children I wanted, but this gave me the freedom to do what I wanted, when I wanted. I didn't have a job, but that gave me the freedom to rest and heal the way I needed to; physically, emotionally, mentally and spiritually. I had access to money that was enough to keep me going. I had good friends around to support me. When I looked at my life from this perspective, my attitude became more positive and I immediately felt happier.

In April, my psychologist said "I think you are ready to begin your spiritual journey" and recommended a personal development course called 'The Turning Point' that was on in May. Well, never a truer word was said and, yes, it was the beginning of a wonderful journey of finding the real me. A journey that still continues today and will last my whole life because there is always something else to learn.

I did The Turning Point weekend. I had only just stopped using the crutches after my third operation, so I was not incredibly mobile for the body work activities, but I participated as much as I could. It helped me start to understand who I was, how I was and why I was like that. It was the beginning of my personal development journey. I also made some great friends who I thought would be in my life forever. Unfortunately that was not the way it worked out, but they were the closest friends I had ever had and they were there for the period I needed them.

In September I began my second course called Mastery which went for 13 weeks. At the beginning of it I took myself off the anti-depressants because I wanted to explore my real feelings without being dulled by drugs. They had done what they needed to do to help me cope and start healing. I also knew I was well supported by my friends and the leaders and support teams on the course.

I had got a job in July as the Asia-Pacific Sales and Marketing Manager of a small software company, which seemed great at first but that didn't last long. When I started work, I also had to wear the hip to ankle brace on my leg for 6 weeks and I remember going into work each day feeling just a bit disabled. It limited my mobility and felt pretty awful, not to mention was not an attractive look, but the concern of my physiotherapist and surgeon that I might never get my leg to go straight again sustained my resolve. I persisted with all I needed to do to get the movement back. I did get most of the flexibility back in my knee … eventually, and then lost some of it again when I had a fourth operation after another ski fall a few years later. Now I just have a stuffed knee – that is the technical term.

Mastery was great for gaining an understanding of how I behaved and responded in relation to others and how they might perceive me. It was very enlightening and helped me to analyse my behaviour and reactions to people and events. The best thing was learning to 'step out of myself' and observe objectively what I was doing and thinking. This was a significant step in my journey. Being able to be the objective observer in my own life helped me to see it from a different perspective and analyse the effect, so I could then have choice in how I responded and what I did.

In the final weekend of Mastery I defined my purpose in life: "To inspire open and honest communication in all relationships, both business and personal, and to travel the world sharing that message." It was at this time I just 'knew' I was meant to be an international speaker helping others transform their lives and their relationships, but had no idea how to get there.

That same final weekend, I also recognised that the job I was in was not in alignment with my purpose as the owner did not have the values I wanted to be around. Well, the very next day I went into work, my boss 'let me go' for no reason. Once again I experienced my incredible ability to create things in my life, although not exactly the way I wanted it to be. The best thing was that I knew it was meant to be and that made it easier to accept and deal with. The next job I had for 11 months until, yet again, I thought it wasn't right for me, only to be made redundant within one month of that thought. I thought I would be better off working for myself after that and sort of fell into subcontracting as a workshop facilitator. That was great fun and took me all over Asia.

The big question I kept asking myself was "how am I creating what is happening in my life and is it how I want it to be?" Being aware of how I behave in life and how I react and respond to people and events was the first step in being able to change what I didn't like. It is a big step, but I think it is only about 20% of the journey. The hardest part is learning how to change and then changing what I didn't like and what didn't get me the results I wanted in my relationships and my life.

To explain how this works, it meant changing the neural pathways in my brain that I had spent my life creating, as that is where my behavioural patterns were defined and recorded. I needed to create new neural pathways of the behaviour I wanted to exhibit. To do that, I needed to choose how I wanted to respond/behave and keep practising that until the new responses became automatic. That is not something one does overnight. It took awareness of when I was behaving in a way I didn't like, discipline to change it to a new way of behaving, and effort to keep repeating the new responses and behaviour. In times of stress I would keep reverting back to that older neural pathway and old behaviour until, after some months of practice, my new neural pathways became the strongest and therefore, my chosen behaviours automatic. This is a lifelong mission to become the best person I can be and we are always creating new neural pathways in our brain so we can constantly change if we choose to.

Through Mastery I had recognised that my marriage was way past its best by date and that it was time for it to end. Even with that acknowledged, my husband had left me with so many unanswered questions because I never got to discuss anything with him. I had to find the answers by myself and for myself. I realised that my marriage ended the only way it could as I had compromised and adapted myself to be content with what I had, even though I felt unfulfilled. For some reason I was prepared to stay in my comfort zone rather than break free and explore on my own. I also recognised that he would never have left me without having someone else to go to, so that was the only way it was going to end, and end it needed to do.

It was the Universe telling me it was time I started working towards my purpose. The Universe also knew I was pretty hard to stop, so it threw everything at me to make me sit on that couch for months on end learning about me rather than going out and distracting myself with other pursuits. When I could, I started doing things I'd always thought about but never actually done because my husband wasn't interested, like dancing lessons (as soon as my knee would let me). I love salsa and Latin American dancing. I did some acting courses and started acting in theatre. I loved acting too and it was something I had always wondered about doing since a child. I had fabulous parties. I went dancing at night clubs and bought new more trendy clothes. I did become a new me. I had a lot of fun times. I also love travelling and went to Europe and the USA a few times, as well as all over Asia for my work.

That doesn't mean my life was all fun and frolics. I had lots of lonely times and I felt a pressure to find someone new so I could still have children with them. This did result in me coming over just a bit desperate I am sure. I found and lost friends to go out with. I felt hurt when people rejected me but I made sure I nurtured myself and got what I needed. I saw a wonderful psychotherapist from then until now. He became like my best friend, coach and confidant as he knew everything about me. I thought "where else can you go to talk about yourself for 90 minutes to a captive audience?" 60 minutes just wasn't long enough for me as I like to talk.

My job situation continued with ups and downs. I knew what my purpose was and that I was going to be speaking to large groups internationally but I had no idea what I was going to speak about and what exactly I was meant to do. It is great to know what your purpose is (and my understanding of it has evolved since then) but that doesn't mean you get to just jump straight into it. It can take a lot of trying different things and constantly evolving who you are and what you do to get there – wherever there actually is. At least that has been my experience.

The following years were filled with exploration to increase my understanding of myself, people and how they relate and what happens in the spiritual world around me. Continuing personal growth has remained a top priority for me and I have done many personal development courses, which I have loved and learned lots in. I also did courses in spiritual healing, psychic abilities, business courses, new concepts and speaker craft. I can't even remember all that I've done. I even have a Certificate in Embodied Relational Dynamics, which sounds pretty funky. I loved this course as I learnt so much about counselling and therapy techniques as well as how the brain works and how we retain the memory of our experiences in our bodies.

Of course I have a large library of shelf help too – some of which I have read and some I still want to read. There never seems to be enough time to do all I want to do. Basically, I am eager to keep learning and following up any opportunities to learn about any topics that resonate with the vibration in me. The day I stop learning will be the day I die, unless I keep learning after that in another world. You never know.

My path has continued to challenge me but then I don't think there is any successful person in the world who has not had their fair share of challenges to get where they are. As they say, when the going gets tough, the tough get going. To be successful, you need to be both resilient and persistent, keep trying different things and to look at challenges as being on the way, not in the way.

I have tried many different paths in my business focus. I have been a marketing consultant, run workshops across Asia-Pacific in partner relationship management and business development, which was a lot of fun and great business, been a sales and marketing manager, lectured at university and delivered sales and professional skills training. At one stage I built an online membership site for spiritual business people but ran out of money before I got it off the ground. That resulted in me having to sell my adored home to "downsize" to something easier (read cheaper) to maintain. That was sad, but I felt like it was time to move on from that house. Yes I have tried lots of things. They have each played a role in making me the person I am and enhancing my experience and knowledge to bring me to where I am today to share the wisdom I have gained.

I have had great times and I have had extremely trying times where from the outside, I seemed to be able to create growth in nothing but debt. Life has not always been easy and my self-confidence has taken much battering, but I have never lost my self-belief in what I am here to do in helping people. I have not yet met the man of my dreams and I never had the children I desired, but that left me free to travel whenever I wanted. Even though I have taken longer than I wanted to achieve the business growth I desire, I can see the constant growth in myself. I am also the eternal optimist and always look for the lesson in everything that occurs.

My journey has been a constant evolution of gaining increasing clarity and ongoing refining of what I am offering as my business. I keep reviewing what I am really good at and also enjoy doing and match that with what people value and need. Finding what you love to do, that increases your vibration, makes you feel great and is aligned with your purpose is the key to life. When you connect into that, you get into flow and then things do seem to just come to you, such as fabulous opportunities that might appear like good luck, but are actually synchronicity confirming you are on the right path.

My business now focuses on showing business leaders and their teams how to move through the communication blockages by getting real with each other. Authenticity has been my significant lesson in my journey through learning to be true to me in how I communicate and relate. Communication and relationships are what life comes down to after all. Life is not really about how many things and toys we can acquire. It is our own growth through relationships with others and how we affect each other's lives that makes the difference to our own happiness.

I wrote my first book a couple of years ago, which was a major milestone in my life and business. It's called 'Get the BALLS to Get REAL – 5 Authentic Strategies to be a Great Communicator'. The BALLS are the 5 strategies; Be open and honest, Adopt an accepting attitude, Lose the blame game, Listen to understand and Stay present. It contains tools and techniques I have used myself to create happy relationships with reduced conflict and for getting outstanding outcomes from difficult conversations by being open and honest.

It was quite easy for me to write the book as The BALLS is the topic I first spoke about in Australia, Canada and the USA and I love writing. The words just came to me easily, as if it was being channelled. It probably was. I based it on my own learnings in life and wrote as if I was coaching the reader, so it contains some coaching style questions to help people understand themselves better. It gives me a real buzz when I can help someone understand themselves and others better, and that is one of the outcomes from reading the book. I love helping people connect to their authentic self, as I have learned to do in my own life.

So with all I have been through, I have learned many life lessons that have made me a better person and helped me pick up the pieces. That is a great feeling of achievement in itself. My persistence and resilience has paid off and will keep paying off as I keep overcoming challenges.

The key to my happiness is to:

- Find and follow your purpose
- Be optimistic
- Keep a positive attitude
- Accept what is
- Keep putting one foot in front of the other when the going gets tough, no matter how hard it is to walk
- Never stop learning

There is always a light at the end of the tunnel, even if you can't see it at the time. Just trust it is there and you will find it. I know. I've been in that dark tunnel and made my way out to the light and it was way brighter and better than before I entered the tunnel. Sometimes you just have to break down to break through.

Janeen Sonsie

About the author

As an international speaker Janeen shows business leaders and teams how to smash through the blockages that stifle their profitability by getting **real** with each other. Armed with Janeen's practical tools, businesses build productive, authentic relationships - leading to lower staff turnover, less workplace squabbling and sabotage, and more engaged people.

Janeen has that rare combination – a technical pedigree with an intimate understanding of the heart of business. During her 25 years in the IT industry – from hands-on technical roles to sales, marketing and management - Janeen worked with some of the globe's biggest names. As a professionally-trained actor, she learned how to tap into her real self, to draw on her own authentic experiences to bring a character to life.

Janeen knows how volatile business can be: she's experienced redundancy, personal loss and the serious impacts of non-existent communication. That's what keeps her fired up to change the way people do business – creating amazing workplaces based on integrity, empathy and respect.

Her qualifications say it all: as well as a Bachelor of Science (Computer Science), Janeen has a Master of Marketing and has lectured in marketing subjects including Customer Relationship Management. Combine that with her vast professional and personal experience, and businesses have access to a power-house of help in growing robust relationships.

Overcoming Polycystic Ovarian Syndrome (PCOS)

Hi my name is Melissa Madgwick and I am on the other side of healing from polycystic ovarian syndrome – naturally.

I have an inspiring story to share with woman around the globe. Women who are suffering with the disease. I want be the voice that helps women to believe they can truly heal with the right knowledge, advice and support. The journey of healing myself from PCOS was a battle like no other. I felt like giving up numerous times. I was in such a dark place that no one could pull me out of the spiral I was in, even my own family. I remember thinking why me? Why am I going through this? I'm looking after myself so why is nothing working? Now I understand why.

Despite the darkness of the PCOS voyage, there was a beautiful gift gained at the end of it all and that was *knowledge.*

I now understand my body so well, I recognise the symptoms when it's out of balance and immediately take the necessary steps to rebalance it. I find myself sharing my story and knowledge on daily basis and it brings me so much joy to see people's lives improving after implementing some advice given.

The valuable information I have gained could only have been learnt through my PCOS experience. If I didn't suffer from the disease and had gone through what I had, I wouldn't be in the position to be able to help others.

This mission in life is much more than myself now. It's to continually inspire and educate the world on the importance of health and self-love. The information I've gained has made such a difference in my own life, I've made it my mission to pass it forward forever.

Foreword

Before doing anything you see in this chapter, speak with your health professional about your ideas. I have not attended medical school. I have not been licensed by any kind of committee or board or government to give any health advice. I have found, however, that most medical doctors have lost sight of the fact that food can be medicine, that humans are not inherently broken and that diseases can be cured by simple, healthful life choices.

I have read hundreds of blogs, and poured many hours of research into the journey of healing myself. You are the captain of your own body and health, and I advise you to weigh my words, your doctor's words and everything you read against your own experience, instincts and knowledge. With my love and light. This is for you.

You are not alone

If you have polycystic ovarian syndrome, you are one of millions of women who suffer from it in the Western world, as I was. Up to 11% of women between 12 and 45 acquire PCOS, and it is considered by some to be the leading cause of infertility. But you can get your life back.

You may have been told there is no way to heal. By 'healing', the medical community means a patented pharmaceutical to address the symptoms. And it's a good thing they haven't got one. The real healing process for PCOS is a change in the behaviours, eating habits and lifestyle choices that caused the problem in the first place. You can achieve 100% recovery! You can get your life, your body, your natural beauty, your womanness and your sex life back! And, yes, you can have babies.

Once you identify the cause or set of causes that conspired to upend your system, you can restore balance in your hormones and turn things around permanently.

In this chapter I'll share a few of my experiences, failures, learning and successes on how to heal from PCOS. I'd like to open your eyes to the diversity of polycystic ovarian syndrome as well as natural interventions for overcoming it. Here's my story.

My PCOS Story

I am a 29 year old woman who is on the other side of healing from polycystic ovarian syndrome – naturally. I was a professional dancer in ballet, tap and jazz for 15 years. I have a university degree and am a passionate entrepreneur.

> *Here's a quick hello from me sharing my story: https://youtu.be/3tfLeopkrJl*

I was someone who had it all— active, sociable, loved life, and was as healthy as anyone can get. However I started experiencing awful PCOS symptoms back in September 2013. It felt as though my life was going down the tube in front of my eyes. I actually hid in my house for 2-3 months because I was so tired, my face and body had broken out in severe acne and I had gained 8 kilos. I had no clue what was happening.

Although I was eating a healthy diet and taking supplements every day, I did not feel healthy. In fact, I was depressed. For eight long years my 'normal life' consisted of terrible acne breakouts lasting three months at a time, terrible menstrual pains and heavy bleeding. My weight was always fluctuating, I had zero sex drive and I was horribly moody. On top of all this, I have an underactive thyroid (only half of the gland is present in my body).

I became so lethargic I did not want to get out of bed. Although my eating patterns did not change, I started gaining weight. Massive, painful pimples appeared all over my chin and jawline, then spread all over my face, chest and back. They were big painful cysts under the skin, not your average pimples.

Thinking it was caused by a hormone deficiency, I went back on the birth control pill. But the acne persisted fiercely. I visited my local doctor and arranged for blood tests on all my hormones. The results came back and I was shocked. My estrogen, progesterone and estradiol levels – all the vital female hormones – were so low they were actually non-existent! The birth control pill was doing nothing.

What was going on? I asked. My doctor had no idea. All she could give me was a suggestion to take oral antibiotics, and to see a dermatologist for my skin issues and go on Roaccutane ®.

The antibiotics didn't work. I decided to see an endocrinologist – a doctor who specialises in women's hormones. After only one consultation, the endocrinologist said my symptoms were screaming out PCOS (polycystic ovarian syndrome). I had heard about PCOS previously. My cousin Leanne from Perth, Australia, was diagnosed years ago with this. I remember distinctly she was told she was unable to have a second child. I felt sick.

As soon as I arrived home, I tackled every resource I could find. I read about women who had overcome the symptoms naturally, including facial acne. I learned how to create a regime of eating healthy, low-GI foods, avoiding toxic foods, taking pharmaceutical-grade supplements and doing the right physical exercises. After only one month, my periods started to regulate for the first time since I was 16. I was getting the nutrients my body needed, and I started to feel better.

My endocrinologist arranged a myriad of blood tests. She wanted to know the levels of every single hormone, and thought we should check if I was coeliac or resistant to insulin. She also arranged scans on my ovaries and thyroid gland. In short, she wanted to know if I was suffering from what she thought.

On the day I came in to see my test results, she told me I had a small clump of cysts in my right ovary. My hormone levels were all out of whack, and my thyroid levels were extremely low. It turned out *she was right*. She diagnosed me with PCOS (polycystic ovarian syndrome) and insulin resistance. She proceeded to write a prescription drug to regulate my insulin levels and then sent me away.

I waited *four weeks* to see her. All I got was a fifteen-minute debriefing. She did not take time to discuss how I was going to cope with all my symptoms. Was there a way to heal? Was there a support group? I needed comfort and support and all she gave me was a prescription that was going to act as a Band-Aid.

The drug was called Metformin, and it was supposed to regulate blood sugar levels. Some women take it and they are fine, but after only two days I became terribly sick and lethargic. I craved sugar and was reaching for anything sweet in sight. This wasn't like me. One afternoon at the local shopping centre, my blood sugar levels were so low I felt as if I was going to pass out in the food court. I bought a salmon wrap and threw it back up within the hour. I discovered Metformin does not agree with sugar or high-carb meals.

After continuing for another two days with horrible side effects, I rang the endocrinologist and decided to ditch Metformin and manage my insulin resistance without drugs.

So many women who have tried Metformin know that it can be a horrible experience, making you lose weight unnaturally and causing low blood sugar levels. I read on hundreds of blogs the experiences women have had with Metformin. It broke my heart. They were suffering. This was when I knew I had to help other women who are trying to find out how to manage and reverse this disease without drugs.

Since January 2014, I have regulated my insulin levels and food allergies with a nutrition-filled diet, I know which foods I'm intolerant to, I meditate, I invest a lot more 'me time' and I keep up a healthy exercise regime.
With normal insulin levels and food allergies addressed, my hormones have readjusted and I have healed myself of PCOS. I do not have any cysts

anymore. I'm healed. I'm back to my healthy self and now it's time for you to help yourself like I did.

I have discovered that the right food and nutrition, a good mindset, a supportive environment, and most of all knowledge are the most powerful tools to heal yourself with PCOS. I'm feeling more alive and I know you will too.

I've broken it down with the top tips many women forget to make and can lead to this disease. I encourage you not to have the 'oh, I've heard that before' attitude. Simply readjust your mindset and think, "How can I apply this new information?"

The Steps to Healing
What do you need to overcome PCOS, like I did? Knowledge is power, so put that first.
Knowledge of who you are, what type of PCOS you have and what your body needs to combat the root cause, is essential to becoming free from hormone imbalances, with the myriad of symptoms that follow.

1. *Know your type.*
Firstly, start with knowing what type of PCOS you have. In my Book 'Heal My PCOS' I discuss the 4 main types of PCOS – what they are and how to manage each. Once the insulin resistance and auto-immune issues were addressed in my case, my PCOS symptoms faded.

2. *I made myself number one.*
I found it takes focus and dedication to heal yourself. I would always put everyone ahead of me and hence the reason why I became sick. You cannot rebalance your hormones if your career is Number One, your spouse or boyfriend is Number One, your education is Number One, your friends are Number One, or your kids are Number One. If you care for other people more than you do for yourself, chances are you will not have the energy to heal yourself. Making yourself Number One is the only way to ensure long term success in your relationships and career. You cannot be much help to your kids, spouse, employer, clients, friends or community if you are not looking after yourself first.

3. *Take charge of your own healing.*
Forget about relying on someone else – your doctor, a friend, a spouse, or a pill – to do it for you. They do not have any power to heal you. The power

lies within you. We are taught to believe there is a magic solution for every medical problem, and the pharmaceutical industry likes to perpetuate this myth. It takes the power out of your hands and prompts you to reach for your wallet. It trains you to see the symptoms and ignore the causes, and this in turn tends to perpetuate the disease itself. This benefits big pharmaceutical companies, not you.

4. Positive mindset and lower your stress.
A positive mindset is so important! When you understand yourself and your body, you'll be able to view everything about yourself in a very different way. You are in control of your body – and stress is a major cause of hormonal imbalances.

Even having PCOS can make you feel stressed out. It can challenge your confidence, self-esteem and feelings of self-worth. You can get worried about losing your boyfriend, husband or partner because you have completely lost all interest in sex. Acne can be painful, and you may worry what people will think when they see acne on your face. I don't blame you for feeling anxious about all these things. I can relate! But the stress is actually unnecessary. The thing is, your current situation is a temporary thing. It will pass, and you will live to tell the tale. So settle in, follow your plan, and watch yourself transform before your very eyes. Enjoy the journey as much as the destination.

My tip is to lower your stress levels is to start meditating for 10 minutes per day whilst doing deep diaphragm breathing. Do not be overwhelmed! Take baby steps until it becomes a habit.

Pursue laughter
When was the last time you experienced a full belly laugh? The kind where you are doubled over, red faced, holding your gut? The kind that makes your belly muscles sore afterward?

This is the laughter that heals. When you laugh, you cannot feel any worry, stress, sadness or anything negative. It releases you – catapults you – from any form of doubt or fear. It brings you back into the present moment where there is no regret about a past and no worry for a future.

Pursue the company of people who make you laugh. Watch funny movies and stand-up comedy. Hang around kids and act silly.

5. Nutrition and supplements.
Your body doesn't need just any food and nutrition; it needs the right food and nutrition. Cut out the empty calories and instead nourish your body with foods that build you up, give you energy and help eliminate toxins. Read about my Low GI PCOS eating plan in my eBook 'Heal My PCOS', then

take the time you need to shop for, prepare, and enjoy eating real food. You'll be surprised how different you feel.

6. Nourish yourself.
Once you have appointed yourself captain of your healing, the primary way to turn your life around is to nourish your body with real food. Although there can be secondary causes of hormonal imbalance, garbage food is the main culprit. And while there are several other factors that will help you heal, real food is your most powerful medicine. Eat real food. Your body loves real food. When you digest natural nutrients that your body can actually use, you feel satisfied, comfortable and energised. Real foods contain digestive enzymes that help you digest the food itself. The more organic or raw, the more digestive enzymes they contain.

Processed foods contain virtually no digestive enzymes. If you eat a tomato, you are giving yourself maximum goodness. When you eat tomato sauce cooked on top of pizza or spaghetti, you are not getting much tomato goodness.

7. Build some muscle.
The best kind of exercise for restoring system balance and optimising your energy is muscle training. Weight training and low body weight can increase the production of stress hormones and, consequently, androgens. It's tougher than stationary bikes and treadmills but the results are fantastic!

You will be truly amazed at what a difference it can mean for your everyday tasks, your energy levels, your appetite, the quality of your sleep and your state of mind. In fact, muscle training is the best type of anti-depressant that exists. Your muscles are sitting there waiting to be used, torn and rebuilt. They are in your body, not something you have to buy. They are one of the most amazing personal assets you have, and simply by building them you can rebuild your strength and your whole constitution.

8. Find the right support.
Your last tool is to find a supportive environment. Participating in a community of like-minded women or supportive friends can help you immensely in navigating your PCOS—and in overcoming it. If you're going through a rough time (like I was), there's nothing like a helping hand to get you through it. Avoid interacting with negative, judgmental people, but instead craft for yourself a network of loving people that will be there for you when you need them.

I've created a loving community at www.healmypcos.com and you can plug in anytime to share your journey.

Your Road to Recovery

You might ask, can simple tools such as new knowledge, a positive mindset, a supportive community and the right nutrition - really improve your life? IT CAN. I am living proof. Every woman is different. PCOS reflect symptoms that SOMETHING is out of balance in your body – largely due to what you are eating, thinking and/or how you treat yourself. I'm excited to share new tips in my new edition and to help you on your road to recovery. The tools that helped me and countless other women are in my Book 'Heal My PCOS'. To be a part of the loving supportive community and to download my eBook 'Heal MY PCOS', please visit: www.healmypcos.com. Stay strong and learn to love the beautiful person you are.

Where I am Today

It's now 2015 and its a few years since my life fell apart when diagnosed with PCOS. I'm more than happy and feel at peace with myself for the first time in my life.

I've moved interstate from Sydney to Perth (where I've always wanted to live), fell in love, I readily focus on my health (as a beautiful gift that I give back to myself), I run a successful branding and digital design business, I am writing more books on various health topics and building a health community on healing people with PCOS, acne and other health related issues I've suffered naturally.

My biggest lesson.

The biggest lesson learnt through all this, which I had to change in order to truly heal and improve the quality of my life, was that at I had to learn to put myself *first.*

Putting ourselves first is the best thing I learned that can help others. It certainly seems to run counter to what I learnt growing up. I was taught to think of others, consider their feelings, and take care of them, while simultaneously being discouraged from doing the same for myself.

But here's the problem with putting others first – you will eventually we run out of energy and your health will suffer, like mine did.

Think of it like this. If a human being is a well, then every time someone draws up water, the water level goes down. Unless there's a source of new water, the well will go dry. The source for human giving is the ability to fill your own well – knowing and fulfilling your own needs before turning attention to helping others. Energy sources will be different for all – some might be spiritual means, relationships, work we love, leisure activities, or anything that brings you peace, joy, and fulfillment. My energy sources are long walks along the beach, healthy foods, love, connection, health, fitness, and being the entrepreneur I know I am. These are main drivers in my life. These are reasons why I get out of bed every day. – I make sure, fill my "love cups", to the point they are over pouring then I am ultimately able to give back to millions more.

Amanda's Testimonial

"Hi Mel – After only 1 month I don't have any cyst's on my ovaries anymore and Mel I have you and your book to thank for that. If it wasn't for you I don't think I would have got back to normal. Now I finally believe I have a chance at getting pregnant. I no longer get bloated when I have a period I no longer crave sugar. I truly hope every women buys your book. I can never thank you enough for all your help. In such a short time I've seen huge differences. Even my hubby says thank you." Amanda Humprhies.

Now it's up to you

If you can take away at least three things from this chapter and put my advice into practice, you will eventually heal yourself from polycystic ovarian syndrome and improve your health. I know I did after three months.

You can rebalance your hormones, get back your menstrual cycle, feel sexy again and bear children. When you know where your most pressing health issues are, you can take the steps laid out in my chapter and my book to overcome these issues through simple lifestyle changes.

I hope my words give you the strength and knowledge you need to act as your own advocate, and the power to create change in your life... starting today. Many women have healed themselves from PCOS naturally, like me, and you can too.

"Give a woman a prescription and she may relief herself for a few weeks, give a women the knowledge and power and she will heal herself permanently". – *Melissa Madgwick.*

I want to hear your success stories

Please get in touch with me and share your journey.
Send your stories to: info@healmypcos.com

Thank you for reading. I wish you all the best in the months moving forward. Happy healing!

With love,
Melissa xoxo

About the Author

Melissa Madgwick is a real 29 year old woman who is on other side of healing from polycystic ovarian syndrome – naturally. She was a professional dancer in ballet, tap and jazz for 15 years. She have a university degree and am a passionate entrepreneur. Life shifted her 3 years ago when diagnosed with PCOS and this is where she took her health into her own hands. For 10 years, her "normal adult life" consisted of terrible acne breakouts lasting 3 months at a time, uncomfortable menstrual pains and heavy bleeding, fluctuating weight, zero sex drive, was always horribly moody and on top of everything, she had an underactive thyroid too. Melissa's life now revolves around healthy living and healing. I'm an avid health advocate who specializes in working with women who suffer from PCOS. Now feeling the best I have in years, I eagerly help others overcome the PCOS disease holistically. My heart signs hearing success stories from the simple shifts in diet, mindset and lifestyle. I'm looking forward to hearing your success stories.

5760557R00126

Printed in Germany
by Amazon Distribution
GmbH, Leipzig